Submachinegun by Giuliano Bruno.
Watercolor, collage, 12 by 18 inches. 2018.

Moon City Review
2019

Moon City Review is a publication of Moon City Press at Missouri State University and is distributed by the University of Arkansas Press. Exchange subscriptions with literary magazines are encouraged. The editors of *Moon City Review* contract First North American Serial Rights, all rights reverting to the writers upon publication. The views expressed by authors in *Moon City Review* do not necessarily reflect the opinions of its editors, Moon City Press, or Missouri State University.

All other correspondence should be sent to the appropriate editor, using the following information:

Moon City Review
Department of English
Missouri State University
901 South National Avenue
Springfield MO 65897

Submissions are accepted at mooncitypress.submittable.com/submit. For more information, please consult mooncityreview.com.

Cover art by Giuliano Bruno
Cover designed by Charli Barnes
Text copyedited by Karen Craigo

moon city press
springfield missouri

Staff

Editor
Michael Czyzniejewski

Poetry Editor
Sara Burge

Nonfiction Editor
John Turner

Fiction Editor
Joel Coltharp

Assistant Nonfiction Editor
Jennifer Murvin

Graphic Narrative Editor
Jennifer Murvin

Assistant Editors

Mackenzie Acup
Emily Aderhold
Shannon Ashley
Sarah Bachler
Abigail Benson
Brandy Clark
Jamie Dougherty
Hannah Farley
Ali Geren
Katelyn Grisham
Amanda Hadlock

Josh Henderson
Mary Henn
Brandon Henry
Breanna James
Emily Joshu
Dane Lale
Brooke Larson
TayMarie Lorenzo
Chloe Massengale
Brooke Matejka

Emily McCormick
Alexis McCoy
Kyle Osredker
Shane Page
Nathan Reames
Michael Rothe
Breea Schutt-Milburn
Taylor Jim Sly
Brooke Spalding
Taylor Vinson
Shannon Wick

Advisory Editors
James Baumlin
W.D. Blackmon
Lanette Cadle
Marcus Cafagña

Table of Contents

Fiction

Poetry

Nonfiction

The Missouri State University Student Literary Competitions

Translation

Contributors' Notes   194

Dana Diehl & Melissa Goodrich

The School Mascot

The teachers are in the break room sharing dirty theories about their school mascot, the Roadrunner.

Ms. Philips stirs chicken flavor into her ramen and says, "He grabbed my ass once, when I was introducing the cheerleaders."

Mrs. Downton wonders if the Roadrunner is inhabited by the ghost of our school's founder.

Dr. Cherez suggests the Roadrunner lives in the rafters of the auditorium like the Phantom of the Opera.

Mr. Chuck thinks about this and then adds, "Do you think he masturbates in there? Inside the costume, I mean."

"Gross, Chuck. Stop," several voices respond.

But Chuck just shrugs and coats his hands in hand sanitizer that fills the room with the sting of alcohol. Several teachers surreptitiously pinch their nostrils shut, count backwards from ten.

No one has ever seen the Roadrunner outside of his costume. No one knows if he is tall or short or beer-bellied or skeletal or mustached or clean shaven. The Roadrunner always leaves just before the end of an assembly, sprints through the double-doors of the gym into the hallway to applause and whoops, wings pumping to the beat of the pep band. Then the halls clog with students, chokes with bodies. The teachers are busy making quiet foxes with their hands, urging lines straight, rescuing dropped Trapper Keepers. By the time they untangle themselves, the Roadrunner is back in the broom closet, propped limply against the water heater amongst buckets and mops and the bags of kitty litter they use when one of their students hurls on the carpet.

Without a body in it, the Roadrunner is stiff and musty. Without a body in it, it still has mesh eye-pockets stiff as kneepads, feathers leather-thick. It's a large and rank cocoon, big and black on the inside.

"No one remembers hiring him," Mrs. Downton says. "He must have started working here before our time."

They imagine their Roadrunner, their Raving, Raging, Roaring Roadrunner, concealing the body of an old man. The firm mesh of the costume holds his decrepit body upright. In his day-to-day life, they imagine he hobbles on aching bunions, uses an electric scooter to move through Sam's Club. But when he places the felt Roadrunner mask over his shoulders, zips the torso to the neck, he feels the pep return to his body, feels like he did as a boy running through his back yard at night, fingers only visible by the silhouettes they make against the stars.

Ms. Cardinal never speaks up during these break room gossip sessions. She stays quiet, Styrofoam cup of tea clasped between her palms, because Ms. Cardinal has a secret.

Between two and three times a week, she visits the Roadrunner's limp, lifeless body in the broom closet. She props a chair under the doorknob, turns off the single hanging bulb, and feels her way through the dark to the Roadrunner. She lowers herself into its soft, felt arms. The Roadrunner has an orange, parted beak reinforced with a cardboard cone that has collapsed a little over the years, givng the Roadrunner's face a drunk, lopsided look. But in the dark, it feels like the soft curve of a valley. The Roadrunner has a soft, white belly and blue wings padded with cotton biceps. Ms. Cardinal likes to prop her cheek against the biceps or the chest, imagines she can hear a heartbeat. Sometimes she runs her hands over the feathers. Sometimes she strokes the plume. She can hear the muted din of student voices in neighboring classrooms, the hush after the stampede towards recess.

Usually she prefers to talk. She whispers secrets into where she thinks the Roadrunner's ears should be (she looked it up once—birds have asymmetrical earholes on the sides of their heads). She talks to the Roadrunner in a soft whisper, like a wife might speak to her husband in bed in the morning, trying not to wake the dog at their feet.

She likes to imagine the Roadrunner as a 65-year-old man, a quiet man who is maybe a little shorter than her but makes up for it with broad shoulders and thick hands. Hands like an Amish farmer's, a man who picks roots with fists instead of machines. She imagines him quiet. Married once, a long time ago, to a beautiful doctor who died tragically while saving a young boy's life in a highway accident. Ms.

Cardinal teaches math, but she has a good imagination. She imagines the Roadrunner running onto the road where the wreck was, seeing his dead wife slumped over the boy with no feet (the highway-accident boy doesn't die, but he loses both of his feet). The Roadrunner re-teaches him to walk because it's what his wife would have done. Something like that. The Roadrunner thinks he's moved on but will sometimes cry in his sleep. The Roadrunner is grateful for the late-in-life love he is finding with Ms. Cardinal.

"I know love is a strong word," she says to the Roadrunner before she leaves the broom closet. "You don't have to say it back."

The teachers have theories about Ms. Cardinal, too.

Mr. Chuck says, "She has crushes on all of the football players. I hear she steals her favorite player's jersey at the end of every year and adds it to a shrine she keeps in her garage."

"She's just lonely," Mrs. Downton says kindly. "She missed her chance at finding a husband."

Dr. Cherez believes that Ms. Cardinal has family, but they all live as historically credible townspeople in colonial Williamsburg. "They're very committed," she says. "They pretend cellphones don't exist."

Today, their conversation turns away from Ms. Cardinal to swimming. One of their school's swimmers, Martin Turner, is rumored to be on track for the 2020 Olympics. He's new to the school this year, and his team has had a winning season.

"Probably taking steroids," Mr. Chuck says, but this is the first time any team at the school has won anything, so no one responds.

The Important Swim Meet is next Saturday, and Martin's teachers have been careful not to assign much homework. They've kept the spelling list simple and water-related this week: chlorine, goggles, filter. They avoid bumping into Martin in the hallways, which is difficult because his upper body is bull-like, boulder-like, enormous for a fifteen-year-old.

"How can someone that *big* swim so well?" Ms. Cardinal mutters, dragging out a recycling bin full of construction-paper scraps.

She doesn't know that Martin Turner wonders the same thing, that Martin Turner used to be a wrestler at his old school until he was expelled for choking someone unconscious in a locker room fight, that Martin Turner didn't mean to be good at swimming when he came here—it was an accident. It was always an accident with Martin Turner.

Mr. Chuck is organizing a Pep Rally for Friday. The cheerleaders have been asked to arrange a special water-themed cheer that will integrate the Roadrunner, the band will be playing a jazzy rendition of "Under the Sea," and the auditorium will be strung with blue streamers and paper fish.

Dr. Cherez hopes an American Olympics recruiter might be in town for the meet, and for the rest of the week, while they're teaching trigonometry or World War II or how to prevent STDs, the teachers will daydream about a future where news reporters seek them out in parking lots, asking, "Did you always know Martin Turner would be a star?" "How does it feel to be *the* Martin Turner's favorite teacher?" They wonder if they'll tell the truth, that Martin was a perfectly polite boy with average grades, or if they'll make up a story about Martin's out-of-control drug use, vodka disguised in water bottles. They imagine painting a word picture of the esteemed, shiny athlete with the troubled past.

Ms. Cardinal is the only one who doesn't wonder. She wipes all of her whiteboards clean and waits for the school to empty.

Ms. Cardinal is working late. She sits at the table in the copier room, the printer humming to a beat that she can tap her foot to, grading last week's fractions test with a blue pen.

Today, she saw a man she didn't recognize in the hallway. He looked shorter than her, stocky, faded blue jeans baggy around the crotch. She watched him through her classroom window for five minutes, watched the way he moved, the way he stood as he chatted with students. She asked herself if he seemed slightly roadrunner-like before remembering that he was the custodian who empties the trashcans during second period.

The Roadrunner is more in disguise outside of his costume than he is in his costume, she thinks. She thinks she also feels this way: Ms. Cardinal the Teacher is someone different from Hannah, who she is at home.

Ms. Cardinal is halfway through her stack of tests to grade when the pen snaps. Blue ink bleeds into her palms, quickly soaks through the papers in front of her. She blinks. The printer is still spitting out papers. She waits for someone to come with a Clorox wipe, with a box of tissues to help her, but the hallways are quiet. The motion-sensor lights have actually gone off. The building is empty.

With her hands held out in front of her, Ms. Cardinal leaves the copier room and makes her way to the broom closet. She knows from her hours spent with the Roadrunner that she'll find a utility sink there and a bar of soap. All the lights in the building are automatic, and they move with her down the hallway, always delayed by just a second. She is always just a few steps ahead of the light, and in those moments of darkness, she wonders if a body lurks in the perimeters. Maybe this time when the lights come on, the Roadrunner will be there with her.

Ms. Cardinal pushes open the door to the broom closet with her toes and lets the light from the hallway guide her to the utility sink. As she scrubs the blue from her hand, she eyes the Roadrunner, splayed against the water heater. The Roadrunner's mesh eyes catch the light. It's easy to imagine that they're real.

She turns off the water. She leaves the door open to the hallway as she drops to her knees and finds her position next to the Roadrunner. She places her head on its shoulders, rolls up her skirt so she can throw one leg across its plush midsection. After a few moments, the lights in the hallways switch off and the closet is all darkness and silence. She wipes her wet hands against the Roadrunner's feathered plume. She wishes it were always like this.

"Hello," she whispers. She remembers she doesn't have to be quiet and says it again, louder. "Hello."

She has a lot to say. She has spent her week imagining what she'll say to the Roadrunner. Every morning, mentally reciting a list of worries and memories to share with him. Lying here next to the Roadrunner, she is not Ms. Cardinal. She is Hannah.

"This morning," she begins. "I ran a red light. I didn't even realize I was doing it until I heard tires screech. What I mean is that I saw the red light but I didn't know to stop. It didn't even occur to me."

The Roadrunner's face feels wet against her cheek. It startles her for a moment until she remembers it's wet from her own wet hands.

"Two days ago," she goes on, "I wanted to break into my neighbor's home while she slept. I know where she hides her key. I walked outside in my pajamas and picked up the key from under the tomato planter and went as far as putting the key in the door, but all

I did was unlock it. I didn't go inside. I left it unlocked and then for the rest of the night worried about a burglar getting in and murdering her."

She pulls the Roadrunner close enough to feel its wing against her pubic bone.

"Sometimes in class, I have to whisper curse words when my back is turned because I know that if I don't, I won't be able to stop myself from screaming them at my students."

It's incredible how one moment she's Hannah and the next moment she's Ms. Cardinal. She puts her legs back together. She smooths her skirt out so it rests respectfully below her knees.

It's incredible how unsafe Ms. Cardinal feels in her body.

Ms. Cardinal was always this way. Even as a teenager, she thought of her emotions as a bowl in her chest with finite size. She'd try to empty it with yoga, with long-distance running, with kissing, with dancing, but nothing would make that bowl spill.

"Are you going to the pep rally after school?" the teachers ask Ms. Cardinal in the breakroom next morning.

She shrugs. She sips tea out of her Styrofoam cup. Up close, she can see that her nails are still rimmed in a thin line of blue ink.

"I hear they're only serving kale and low-fat yogurt for lunch today," Dr. Cherez says. "It's supposed to help swimmers remain buoyant."

Mr. Chuck says, "Mrs. Downton excused Martin from class today so he could go get a deep-tissue massage in preparation for the race."

Ms. Cardinal smiles with her coworkers. Ms. Cardinal isn't going to the pep rally tonight because she is tired of watching the Roadrunner dancing and jumping and shimmying from afar. She's tired of wondering if he is catching her eye, if somehow the man in the costume senses the moments they've stolen together.

Tonight, she's decided, she will meet the Roadrunner.

She sips her tea. She picks blue ink from under her nails.

Ms. Cardinal waits in the darkened broom closet, hidden behind the water heater. She hasn't decided if she wants the Roadrunner to see her when he arrives.

She can hear the assembly hall full of voices. The voices move like a swarm of insects, like an airplane engine, loud.

She imagines the door to the broom closet turning, imagines watching that neck unzip, that mask come off, the slow turn and reveal of a face.

But even when the stomping on the bleachers stops and the loud ruckus of hallwaying ends, he doesn't come. No one is coming. She falls asleep in the closet, behind the water heater, that way.

She is sore and bedheady and embarrassed when she wakes in the night. She pulls open the closet door and the motion sensor lights click on a moment later.

On the ground in front of her, in the hallway, is the Roadrunner. Face down, body splayed, not snoring. She crouches, she listens and leans over the mouthpiece, feeling for heat. "Oh my god," she says and reaches for the zipper, reaches inside to find a pulse.

The thing is, there isn't a body in there. It's empty, as it always was. It's empty and yet it was posed like death, like it was dead, like whatever it was that was in there left.

She props the costume up against a locker. It starts to tip. She straightens it up.

Ms. Cardinal looks at it sideways, cocking her head. She unzips the neck fully. She lifts the mask over her own head. It smells like mint and dog and maybe aftershave. She swivels her head, enjoying the strangeness of a beak. Then she steps into the body of the Roadrunner, stretches her arms inside the wings, takes a moment to adjust to her new proportions.

In costume, her body disappears. She becomes the Roadrunner. She closes her eyes and feels her body disappearing like evaporating water.

She is plume, she is mesh eyes, she is soft knees.

She is three-toed feet. She is flightless wings.

She walks into the closet, where she will feel safer, where she can explore this new body. Once in the dark of the closet, she realizes how tired she still is. She yawns, her yawn hidden by beak. She falls asleep standing. It feels natural now that she's a bird.

When she wakes, she is a body under bright, white light. Someone announces over the loudspeakers THE ROOAAAAAAAAAAADRUNNEEEEEERRRRR, and now she is doing cartwheels and sit-spins. She could never do cartwheels before, and this is not a dream. She is pumping her wings and tumbling into the cheerleaders like a bowling ball knocking down pins.

She tries to stop, but she doesn't stop. She thinks about leaving the gymnasium, running down the hallway to her old classroom, standing in the corner under the flag, where she can't be seen from the door. Instead, she skips to the drumline, pounds her wing-fists against the bass drum. Instead, she inspires the teachers to start the wave.

She is doing somersaults across the three-point line when the gymnasium goes silent. No one is looking at the Roadrunner. Everyone's looking at the open gymnasium doors. She turns to look, too. A crowd of boys is entering the room. They're wearing identical, blue tank tops and gym shorts, and Martin Turner is leading them. Martin Turner, unsmiling and big-armed. Upon seeing him, she feels a surge of school pride, so much pride that she feels compelled to do a handspring.

When the swim team has fully entered the gym, it's like a string has snapped inside her. She isn't tired, exactly. Not sad, exactly. She is just done. The school screams for the swim team, and she runs away, out of the gymnasium, down the hallway to the broom closet.

She hangs herself up against the water heater like a jacket.

It's not a bad life, being the Roadrunner. She can listen to the drip of the closet sink for hours. And now, she's the one they cry to. She didn't realize how many people come to the Roadrunner to talk. She likes to feel needed. She likes the press of cheeks against breastbone. She likes the sobbing sound that teachers make.

Mrs. Downton's brother is in jail for peeping on a woman in a changing room.

Ms. Philips can't have sex anymore without having an accompanying panic attack.

Dr. Cherez wakes up to a spider crawling in his ear.

Mr. Chuck spanked his toddler son for the first time and hated that it felt cathartic.

She remembers a time when this would have all been terrifying to her, but she's not scared now, and so those used-to feelings don't matter.

She didn't realize it sucks the body out of you, this listening.

☾

One day, Martin Turner comes in. It's the day before the meet or the day after. It's hard keeping track of time when your body dissolves and reappears like an accident, like every time you're in your body you're running a red light.

Martin Turner crumples over the sink and vomits, masking the sound with running water.

He's dripping in his swim trunks. He's barefoot and fresh-shaved—all his hair, his face, his arms, his legs, his chest, which she realizes is bare. He vomits and cries a little into the sink. Every part of him is leaking.

Martin Turner says, "This fucking school."

The Roadrunner tries to straighten up inside her body, tries to take on the posture for hearing. Maybe she succeeds, because Martin Turner glances over in her direction. His eyes are red and swollen, and the Roadrunner remembers then that he is just a kid.

Martin Turner wipes his nose and mouth with the back of his hand.

"So this is where they keep you," he says.

He takes a step towards her. He picks her up by her wings. The Roadrunner had imagined herself heavier, is surprised her body is light enough for a boy to lift. Martin Turner looks her in the mesh eyes. "Let's take a drive," he says.

Martin Turner props up the Roadrunner in the passenger seat of his pickup. No seat belt, so when Martin's driving, the Roadrunner slides across the seats, folds forward at the waist, beak nestled in an empty coffee cup, legs akimbo.

It's hard being in a body like this. It's hard when you can't see, can't move the pieces you are made of.

Martin Turner drives for hours. He stops somewhere for french fries, and the Roadrunner can smell the grease of a hamburger and feels the grime of salt when Martin rubs his hands on her like a towel. He pulls over somewhere. She realizes she's become the McGuffin in a story she didn't catch the beginning of. She is the white dress stained with red wine. She is the gun that has to go off.

Martin Turner parks and the car goes quiet. He opens his door and pulls the Roadrunner out after him, pulls her by the plume. He lets her body drop onto the ground. She feels the tar on the pavement stain her fabric skin.

They are in a parking lot at the edge of a lake. Grass. Lake. Mountains. Sky. Everything is a shade of dark blue.

"I think I'm going to put you on," Martin Turner says. He unzips her neck. He steps inside her body, what's left of it. He steps inside.

She is waiting for the lights to come on, for the auditorium full of students to roar. If enough people cheered right now, she thinks she could wrestle him out, thinks she could put herself back together again.

Martin Turner lifts the Roadrunner's head from the ground and puts it over his head.

She's not sure what she expected. Part of her is surprised that her old body isn't still there, isn't still inside her new Roadrunner skin, shrunken up and sleeping like the smallest piece of a Russian nesting doll. Part of her is surprised that the moment Martin Turner put on the costume, she didn't poof out of existence.

In her skin, Martin moves towards the water. He is awkward as the Roadrunner. His arms are too big for the wings. His torso is too short. He tastes like chlorine and gum and booze.

The Roadrunner wonders what happened to the other Roadrunner. The Roadrunner she cried to before she became it. Where did he—or she—go? Is he still here, still here under the mask someplace where she can't find him? Martin Turner is becoming more confident in the costume. He is running now, running towards the dark-blue lake, which means she is running, too. The Roadrunner remembers real running, real roads, the heavy slap of her sneakers into the pavement, the way she kept a Swiss Army knife in her pocket, knowing any moment someone could tackle you, drag you behind a tree or into an alley—it wouldn't even have to be a shadowy place, knowing that if you are a running woman, you are as easy to see as neon, you are a spotlight, a cymbal crash, open as a door with no key.

At the edge of the lake, Martin stops.

"Who am I winning for?" he says, and his voice is absorbed into the plush of her head. His voice becomes her for a moment.

Then he steps. She doesn't feel the water, but she feels its weight. The water rushes inside of her, rushes to fill the space between her skin and Martin's. Martin keeps stepping until they are submerged up to the chest.

"Ra, Ra, ROADRUNNER!" Martin howls into the mask.

Then Martin and the Roadrunner dive. They plow their arms through the water. The Roadrunner feels what it feels like to be an Olympics-destined swimmer. She feels herself filling with water. But she doesn't notice Martin Turner filling with water, too. She already lost her body, so it's hard to empathize all the pockets filling in his.

He is still kicking, still plowing, as they drift down to the bottom of the lake. It is gray down here, not blue. Algae rises around them like streamers. Martin is clutching at their neck with their wings. He thought he wanted to die, but he doesn't, not really. It was only a fantasy he thought he'd believed.

His heartbeat is so fast she can hardly stand it. She wishes he'd lay his head against her and explain what led him here. But she knows he'll keep fighting, she knows that against all odds he'll break free, because that is what Martin Turner does. He'll make it to the swim meet, he'll do his best, the Roadrunner way.

Charles Harper Webb

Remove Child Before Folding

the label on our stroller scolds. *Harmful*
   if swallowed screams the glittering spoon
I troll for trout which, lucky for me, can't read.
  Seeing, on a Superman cape, *Warning:*
Does not enable you to fly, and on a can

of almonds, *Product may contain nuts,*
   I want to bellow, "Nuts to you!" But
a judge bankrupted a restaurant that sold
  oysters without advising, *Do not*
eat the shells. And who wouldn't want

to paint on a son's HOG, *Do not ride—*
   and if you do, never with thugs.
What husband wouldn't stamp,
  in red letters, across Sven-the-tennis-coach's
strapping chest, *Avoid all contact with skin?*

Why not inscribe on every newborn's heart,
   Stopping can lead to injury or death,
and before flying, pull on *Unlawful*
  to drop underwear? Why not tattoo
yourself, *Do not shoot with hard projectiles,*

or force to inhale water. Do not infect,
   abuse, thwart, disappoint, impede self-
actualization of. Serve favorite foods, but not
  in excess. Never fail to press your lips lovingly
here.

Loria Mendoza

Black Fish

The first fish you catch is small and full of fingernails.
You arrange them in a circle by size and moon-phase resemblance
and bait your hook with its head.
The next fish is heavier, silver and carnivorous.
When you cut it open you find a bundle of bloody flags.
You use your knife to cut hundreds of tiny crosses into the fabric
and cast the net your repetitive hands have made.
You cast it far
and wide
and up.
For an instant in the air, you see it clearly.
You can't help but notice the shape of it:
the sliding expression of a mouth breathing out your verdict.
The fish it catches spits out thin blue coins,
your winter wages.
We were all fish once, surely you know this.
You're certain of it
though you don't remember.

Donald Illich

Against Hammers

The hammers sing, but we can't hear them.
We're busy counting money in our accounts,
saving for a regimented vacation of fun.
We're playing with the bones of our bodies,

near-crashes, accidents in the mountains.
We're calculating the words we can say
to our children, remain cool in their eyes.
The hammers don't care. They smash

through rock like it's heaven. Crushing
blocks on the street, they prepare the way
for trucks to be captured by driveways.
Their voices are shaking through our skeletons,

but we try to ignore them. Better no hammers,
then the nails would finally be freed, no reason
to penetrate hands, feet. A cross would be
a cross. We'd forget how to pray for anything.

Virginia Watts

When Christmas Dawns

The Sears and Roebuck Company kept our wishes glossy. Whenever I taste bologna, the pale pink kind, I think of the 1968 Christmas Wish Book. I am eating my lunch and searching in a wishing well at the same time, flipping catalog pages like song selections inside a diner's tableside jukebox. A lot of catalog pages are dedicated to nightwear: pajamas that resembled clown costumes, robes and gowns. Spice racks, glass bottles with sailing ships corked inside, cuckoo clocks, punch bowls, their cups hooked around perimeters like an expectant flock, TV dinner table trays galore.

My two older brothers and I are contemplating an electric shoe polisher to supplement our father's standard gift set of Old Spice Cologne, English Scent, not Lime. My mother's Christmas is decided: a pale blue, quilted robe and a dainty, silver Bulova wristwatch. My oldest brother, Curt, has circled the Big Bowl Electric Football Game. That choice proved disappointing. The players ran jerky, slows patterns. Instead of tackling, they ran into each other and toppled over like miniature, scowling bowling pins.

My brother Mark is the owner of too many microscopes and telescopes already, according to our parents, so he has a forced wish: a tabletop planetarium. The accompanying, four-foot plastic dome promises a realistic representation of stars and constellations. The planetarium was more of a disaster than the football field. No one considered that the ceilings inside our ranch house were too low to hang a structure as big as a baby elephant's shoulders. The night sky would never consider leaving such a perfect place, anyway.

With Christmas around the corner, I nibble winter, weekend lunches, jettisoning through lawn croquet sets, walkie-talkies, a Pedal Power bicycle with the banana seat, pages of View Masters, "practically kid-proof" phonographs, and zithers. The children in the catalog look like Dick and Jane from the school readers and their supporting cast: Baby Sally, Mother, Father, and the Dog Spot. There is Jane, seated behind a lighted vanity brushing her hair, pushing a battery-powered vacuum cleaner, ironing on a board just her height, smiling at plastic food inside the refrigerator of an All Steel Avocado Kitchen Set.

I yawn over the pages: a French provincial doll bassinet, a beauty school to teach me how to style hair, musical jewelry boxes spinning ballerinas. I know a wetting, Dy-Dee baby doll won't delight me. I'm not interested in hair, mothering, housekeeping or cooking. I am trying to be mod like Barbie and her friends Stacey and PJ, and in 1968, all of a sudden, out of the blue, there is something else. Barbie can talk for the first time. There is my perfect Christmas wish without a doubt! According to the catalog: "You never know what Barbie's going to say!" Talking Barbie winks back at me as I circle her a hundred times. I punch my wish right out of the catalog page and set her free.

Talking Barbie arrives peeking from my Christmas stocking wearing a coral bikini with a white plastic belt and a silver mesh cover-up tapping the tops of her thighs. She has bright coral cheeks, coral lips and rooted eyelashes, thank god! What does she say to me?

"Would you like to go shopping?"
"I love being a fashion model."
"I have a date tonight!
"What should I wear to the prom?"
"Let's have a costume party!"
"Stacey and I are having a tea."

Those were six, fairly disappointing statements that Christmas morning, but the doll was dewy pretty. The problem was, I was seven in 1968: no prom, no fashion, no dates, no mall shopping with friends yet. That Halloween, I had gone trick-or-treating dressed as Clara Barton, not to a party. The last statement worried me the most. It made Stacey and Barbie seem poor, like they had to share the same teabag: not "having tea," or "having a tea party." It worried me like the future song "Squeeze Box" by The Who would worry me. Mama has a squeezebox. Daddy never sleeps at night. I know they aren't singing about a variety of accordion. I have nothing against the "in and out" as long as Mamma is really "in" and doesn't want more sleep at night.

In 1968, there was something else though, something really awesome that blew in from Mattel Land and made up for the fact that Barbie and I weren't going to talk to each other. Talking Barbie was more than a voice box, a coral bikini, coral cheeks, and coral lips. Coral also means a lobster's ovaries. Mattel hadn't gotten to ovaries yet, but for the first time in history, Mattel had separated the fingers on Barbie's tiny hands.

So let's just say Barbie is fifteen years old. She is at a party with Ken who is seventeen. Ken is wearing a shiny, white tuxedo jacket and black dress slacks. He has a golf handicap, too, and everyone is drinking "not tea," but not too much "not tea" to erase memory like a wet sponge does a blackboard, more like an eraser when it needs to be clapped. You still see the ghost thoughts watching you on an erased blackboard.

Now, in 1968, when Ken puts his hand over Talking Barbie's coral mouth, she can raise her arm and separate her index finger from her middle finger and stick them straight into the middle of Ken's eyeballs and then since there was probably a Talking Ken, too, Ken can call out in blind pain and Barbie can get out from under the weight of him and off the bed and walk out the door.

In 2018, you can purchase a 1968 mint condition Talking Barbie on eBay for $248, but they are extremely rare. Most of these vintage dolls have no limbs. The 1968 Talking Barbie is prone to toppling limbs, and the vast majority are mute now, but not all of them. Some still talk when you pull the magic string on the back of her neck.

Ian Denning

Drawing of a Spaceship Breaking Up Over the Moon

The day before my brother's twelfth birthday, my dad brought me to the toy store in the mall. It was September. School nights were dark and quiet, and I was happy to escape the house.

"You're my advisor," Dad said and reached over and cuffed my shoulder. "We'll find him something good." I didn't care what toy my brother got. I knew he wouldn't let me play with it, and I was as selfish as any ten-year-old, lost deep within my own private worlds.

I had already seen everything in the toy store. I walked through the tropical frog colors of the squirt-gun aisle while Dad compared three remote control cars with a clerk. *How much juice are we going to get out of a 7.2-volt battery?* I dug my hand into the bin of twenty-cent rubber dinosaurs—I loved the dull prick of their horns against my fingers and the clean latex smell they left behind—and then I saw the sign for the Super Toy Spree Sweepstakes. "How many toys can you grab in five minutes?" it asked.

"Dad, can I sign up for this?"

Dad, busy with the clerk, said, "Sure, Matt, go ahead." I filled out the postcard and slipped it into the slot in the cardboard stand. Dad bought the most expensive of the three RC cars.

Neil was having a party with his friends at a paintball field that weekend, so it was just me and Mom and Dad around our kitchen table to watch him blow out the candles. Neil's face didn't change when he opened the RC car. "Check out the suspension," Dad said. He traced his finger across the oversized shock springs on the box. "Very rugged. I thought we could take it out to the baseball fields this weekend."

"Sure, Dad," Neil said and slid it aside so he could tear into Mom's present. It was a sweatshirt from the Gap, the brand name printed in distressed block letters, folded as carefully as a flag.

"I thought you should hit middle school in style," Mom said.

Dad held it up against Neil to check the fit. "Looks pretty swanky."

"Yeah, real *swanky*," Neil said, the mockery in his voice a shade too light for Dad to pick up. He grabbed the shirt and returned it to its box. "It's perfect, Mom."

After cake, I locked myself in my room. Who was excited to get a shirt for their birthday? An RC car was way better. If I won the Super Toy Spree Sweepstakes, I'd build a whole fleet of RC cars.

I flopped across my bed and opened my notebook to the first fresh page. Over the last few weeks, I had filled twenty pages with epic space battles: raked-back capital ships and fighters like darting stilettos, an insectoid alien race inspired by a hornet I had traced out of an encyclopedia, incandescent laser fire and budding explosions. I had designed all the ships myself and filled the back pages with histories and descriptions of heroic space captains and tragic alien warriors bound by their race's strict warrior code. I flipped to the drawing I had started yesterday, an alien hive-ship exploding above a moon, and kept sketching.

In their bedroom down the hall, my parents were arguing. I could hear their "T"s and "D"s clipping through the walls. I heard Dad mention my brother, Mom say the words "middle school boys" and spit my father's name, but I couldn't hear the details. I switched off my lamp and let my room fill with the light of the moon, filtered blue by my galaxy curtains. I put my ear against my pillow to dampen Mom and Dad's argument, and I stared at the glow-in-the-dark sticker of Saturn I had stuck to my desk drawer, reduced, in the dark and its own fading phosphorescence, to a stain of light.

Years after my parents' divorce—after Neil got his MBA and worked on Wall Street and after my art school and grinding on part-time design gigs finally paid off—my brother moved back to the Portland suburbs with his family and into a house identical to the one in which we grew up. The house was in a cul-de-sac a few miles from our old home, but it must have been built by the same contractor. Same floor plan, same canted ceilings, same feeling of expensive suburbia I had grown up with: a heaviness to the walls and doors and the air itself.

I didn't know why Neil chose the house, but then I didn't know why Neil did anything. We had even less in common as adults than we'd had as children. I was softening into my mid-thirties; Neil, with his paleo diet and thrice-weekly CrossFit, looked more and more every year like he was carved out of oak. I lived in a studio in Seattle clogged with dirty laundry and takeout boxes; Neil and his wife's home had been photographed for the lifestyle-and-leisure section of *Portland Monthly*. Neil played golf; I played role-playing games. We only ever talked on birthdays and holidays.

I went down at Christmas to visit Dad and wound up staying in Neil's guest room. Walking through his house felt like watching a movie and realizing halfway through you've seen it before. Mom and Dad's room was Neil and his wife's. Mom's office had become Neil's office, the desk in a different corner but the stacks of papers and notes and the whiff of workaholism almost identical. My room, pink and scattered with princess dolls and coloring books, belonged now to Sarah, Neil's four-year-old daughter. Seeing my childhood excavated like that made me feel tired. I should take a cab, I thought, sleep in the airport, catch a red-eye. I should get away from this.

Instead, I hid from the other adults with Neil's kids in the basement playroom—same old playroom, newer electronics—and played video games. My nephew Hank worshiped me because I worked for the company that made his favorite video-game series. His parents didn't let him have my games—too violent—so he had to play them at his friends' houses.

"So you get paid to draw aliens?"

"Pretty much," I said. "Do you still like to draw?"

"Sometimes. Do you draw the aliens or the Marines?"

"Little bits of everything," I said. "I'm an assistant to the art director, who's like the boss. He has a picture in his mind about how the game is going to look, and I help him make it look like that."

"That's so cool," Hank said.

It was mostly answering emails and sitting in meetings, but you can't tell a ten-year-old that. "Yeah, it's very cool," I said. "I got my own project on the last game. I made the alien home-world."

Hank frowned. "I don't think I've gotten to their home-world yet."

"You will," I said.

Upstairs, the phone rang. I could tell by Neil's voice when he answered that it was Mom. Sarah and Hank must have known, too, because they bolted upstairs—they loved Grandma. I stayed, sitting cross-legged in the room that both was and was not my childhood basement, thinking about the ancient constellation of my family.

At a gaming conference in Boston a few years ago, I met another Super Toy Spree Sweepstakes winner at a bar. He was a pop-culture blogger and looked like all the other pop-culture bloggers swarming the convention hall: button-down shirt, expo badge, expensive-looking glasses—there was no evidence that as a child he had been touched by absurd fortune.

"My dad filmed my reaction when they told me," he said. "I lost it. Like, I totally lost it. N64 Christmas Kid-level apeshit. It's on YouTube. What's your Twitter handle? I'll tweet you the link."

I wished I could have shared a similar experience, but that's not how I reacted. I didn't find out I had won until January, almost four months after I entered. I was working on my space battles when Mom called both me and Neil downstairs.

Mom and Dad were sitting stiffly at the kitchen table, both frowning. I could tell by the static gloom in the atmosphere that they'd been fighting again. Neil didn't sit when I sat, and the expression on his face was both slack and tense, like he was waiting for a blow and already pretending it didn't hurt. "Sit, Neil, it's OK," Dad said, and Neil scraped out his chair and fell into it.

Mom sighed and said, with no preamble, "Matt won the Super Toy Spree Sweepstakes."

"I did?" I said.

Neil's face changed. He flushed and sat up. "That thing from TV?"

"The network is flying us all down to California next week," Mom said. "I already talked to your schools and got you excused."

"Can you beat that?" Dad said. "Toys, surprise vacation, your first time on a plane. Pretty exciting, right?"

I wanted to jump up and yell, but Neil and Mom were both so obviously unhappy, and Dad's amusement so stilted and tense, that I only nodded. Before I could think of something to say, Neil cut in. "Why did Matt get to put his name in and not me?"

Mom turned to Dad and crossed her arms. "Yes, David, why?"

"He signed up when we were out buying your birthday present, I think," Dad said. "Remember, your RC car?"

Neil started trembling. "So Matt wins the Super Toy Spree Sweepstakes and gets all the toys he wants and I get a shitty remote control car."

"Neil, language!" Mom said and turned to me. "Matt, you will share the toys you win—all of them—with your brother."

"Who else is he going to share them with, anyway?" Neil said. "It's not like he has any friends."

"Neil!" both my parents said at once, but Neil had already stood up and stomped out of the kitchen, toward the stairs. The door to his room slammed.

"Anyway, we're excited for you," Dad said. "And we're excited to do it as a family." He squeezed Mom's hand when he said it and she looked away.

That night, alone again in my bedroom's blue glow, I listened to Dad's footsteps on the stairs. I could hear my brother yelling through the walls, "It's not fair, it's not fair, it was for my birthday," and I could hear Mom in his room, murmuring to him. How strange that my good luck could wound my brother like that—my brother who didn't even like toys anymore. I wormed down into my blankets, feeling warm and ripe with good news.

We had to get up at five in the morning to get to the airport on time. Dad let me have the window seat, and I rested my head against the glass during takeoff. I watched the runway wane beneath us, the Columbia River narrow to a gray band, the houses of Troutdale and Washougal shrink to playset size, then to Micro Machines, and I thought about kicking through them like Godzilla or Super Geon in *King of the Monsters 2*. Anthills collapsing beneath my Adidases.

Los Angeles was warm and gray, and we had to ride in a cab for an hour to reach the hotel. Me, Neil, and Dad were all sharing one room—the biggest hotel room I've seen to this day, three beds in two rooms, with a bathroom half the size of my room at home—and Mom had her own room across the hallway. "Hope you don't mind me bunking up with you," Dad said while he dragged our luggage to the closet, "Your mom's got a lot of work to do while we're here."

Neil flopped on the bed and stared at the ceiling. "Sure she does."

Dad turned to me. "Anyway, us boys get to rough it in our bachelor pad," he said and grunted like Tim Allen on *Home Improvement*, which always made me laugh.

The network producer, a lady in a suit, picked us all up in an SUV and drove us to the toy store I would run through. "We're going to bring in a bunch of local kids to cheer you on, Matt, get you really pumped!" she said as we walked through the glass doors into the cool lift of the air conditioning. "Right now, the idea is to walk through the store and pick out the things you want ahead of time, sound good?"

Mom and Neil, who had both been in a black mood ever since we left, were at the Gap. I could finally let my excitement show. "It sounds great!" I crowed, and all the adults laughed.

I had spent a week reading newspaper ads and watching commercials, and I had a list of everything I wanted. Remote-control cars, Batman action figures, a new bike, Teenage Mutant Ninja Turtles, the Nerf Crossbow, the Nerf Ballzooka, the Super Soaker XP 250, Power Rangers Megazords, Laser Challenge, at least a dozen Super Nintendo games, a Sega Genesis. As I walked through the aisles with the producer and Dad, I felt anticipation and greed rising in me like gases.

Mom and Neil came back from shopping. Mom was frowning at a work document she had printed out in the hotel. The producer asked her my clothing sizes for wardrobe and she pulled at my neckline and the butt of my pants to get at the tags. I was too excited to be embarrassed.

"I don't get cellular reception in here, so I have to run outside real quick," she said. "Neil, do you have anything you want Matt to get for you?"

"No," Neil said then added quietly, "a new bike. A Huffy."

"Totally!" I said, forgetting for a moment what a dillweed my brother had been about the Super Toy Spree and honestly wanting to help him get a new bike. He must have thought I was being sarcastic, because he scowled at me and didn't talk at all on the drive back to the hotel. He and Mom were silent, but Dad asked me what I was going to get, and I named toy after toy after toy.

☾

"So, what did you bring us for Christmas?" Hank asked without a trace of shame.

Hank had just assembled a *Star Wars* Lego on the couch, and Sarah and I were coloring on butcher paper spread out on the basement floor. The adults were upstairs, watching a Seahawks game.

"Did you bring me a pony?" Sarah asked.

"No, it would have been hard to bring a pony down on the train from Seattle. Amtrak frowns upon ponies."

"Grandma gave me four ponies last year," Sarah said. "They're in my room."

"That's awesome," I said. Mom spoiled Neil's kids from afar. Last year, she flew them down to see Disney on Ice at the Oracle Arena. I wondered if she would do the same for my kids, if I ever had any.

Hank put his new Lego on the shelf with the others and dropped the instruction manual into a drawer full of spare parts. These kids were so clean. Growing up, our house was littered with Neil's soccer gear and plastic spaceships and action figures, but Neil and Celia had managed to train their children to be neat. "Give me a hint about my present," Hank said. "Is it your game? Your newest one?"

"I don't think your mom and dad would be down with that," I said.

Hank went to the shelf and adjusted his Legos. He was blushing. "I know."

Upstairs, Neil groaned at something one of the football teams had done. Sarah had gone back to drawing brown arcs upon arcs. There was a winter light in the basement playroom, a glowing in the blinds that reminded me of December afternoons when I was a kid, that pre-Christmas ache in your mouth, the mystery of gifts.

"I know you know," I said and tried to phrase my thought in a way that Sarah wouldn't understand. "But the next time I visit, I wouldn't be surprised if a certain video game were to make its way into a certain boy's backpack and from there to a certain friend's house."

Hank looked up. "Really? Uncle Matt, I—wow, thank you!"

"Don't thank me, I haven't done anything."

I knew I was being irresponsible and that Neil would be furious if he found out, but screw it. Uncles are supposed to funnel their nieces and nephews cool stuff their parents don't want them to have. It would make the kid happy, and aren't childhoods supposed to be happy?

☾

I couldn't sleep the night before the Super Toy Spree. The hotel room didn't have the familiar contours and numinous blue light of my room back home, and the air felt different, the way water tastes different when you travel to a faraway city. I lay awake, imagining myself sweeping toys into the shopping cart, the cameras dollying back to give me room, local kids screaming my name.

"Matt," Neil whispered. I looked at him, at the door that led to dad's room in the suite, then back to him. "Matt, I know you're awake."

"What," I said.

My brother sat up in bed and stared at me. "I've seen your gay space drawings."

"You were snooping in my room?"

"I wasn't snooping," Neil said. "You left them out on your bed, dumbass."

I stayed quiet, and he scooted over in his bed so he was as close to mine as he could get. Only the end table and the green numerals of the clock separated us.

"You're so weird, just sitting in your room and drawing your gay space drawings all the time."

"They're not gay," I said, but I was blushing. Nobody at school ever talked about locking themselves in their rooms to draw, let alone draw science fiction. My hobby was strange and I knew it.

Neil flopped sideways onto his pillow. "I hate that I have to be here to watch you win a bunch of stupid toys," he said. "Mom hates being here, too."

"No, she doesn't."

"She does. She hates being here," Neil said. He got out of bed and stood over me, clenching and unclenching his fists. "And I hate you."

Neil was a fuzzy darkness against the dark of the room. I thought he might hit me, but my comforter was warm and the air conditioning was humming the room empty, and I didn't care. I knew in that moment that my brother really did hate me, and I didn't care about that, either. I hadn't done anything wrong except for like the things I liked. I crossed my arms, looked up at him, and said, "If you keep saying that, I won't get you any toys."

"I don't want your stupid toys." He leaned down, put his face right in mine, and said, "I want you to die."

"You want that Huffy?"

"No, I just want you to *die*."

"Too bad," I said and turned away from him.

Neil grunted and climbed back into his own bed. After a while, his breathing evened out and I knew he was asleep. I would get him his Huffy—even if he punched me in my sleep, even if he called my space drawings gay a million times, I would get him a Huffy. I would do it to prove that I was better than him. And to prove that he was my brother, even if I wasn't his.

Hank pedaled a lazy and practiced loop around the cul-de-sac. I stood with my hands tucked into the pockets of my peacoat, looking out for cars and watching Sarah scrawl pink and yellow arcs of chalk on the asphalt. Dad, Neil, and Celia were at the mall, buying the last of the Christmas presents, and I was babysitting.

"You should come down and visit more often," Hank said. "Seattle is really close."

"I should. I really love seeing you guys."

He looped around again, tried a bunny hop, wobbled and regained equilibrium. He had his dad's easy athleticism, that little-boy fearlessness I'd never seemed to possess. "Dad doesn't get what you do. He called you 'frivolous.'"

"Frivolous!" I laughed. "That's a very Neil word."

"Yeah, but he doesn't get it," Hank said.

But he did. We both did. We understood frivolity and work and what thirty years of being brothers can do to people. We understood that divorce turns kids into other people or maybe into the people they had secretly been all along, like Link going through the magic mirror in *Zelda*. You think you're a hero, but in the dark world, you're just a helpless pink rabbit. A frivolous thing. "Your dad and I are coming from two very different places," I said.

"What do you mean?"

"Some people use toys and video games and science fiction to fill a gap," I said. "What's frivolous to one person can be everything to another."

"He doesn't get it," Hank said again. He managed to buck his bike up on the rear wheel and hop twice before he lost his balance and had to put his feet down. "Anyway, it would be cool to see you more."

"I'll put a date on the calendar before I leave," I said as Neil's car rounded the corner into the cul-de-sac. "I promise."

☾

I won $10,586-worth of toys from the Super Toy Spree, including new bikes for me and Neil and everything on my list. Most of it disappeared over the next few years, all ten-and-a-half thousand dollars of it: lost in one move or another, given away, donated to Goodwill, broken. Today, the only things I still own are the video games.

The network shipped everything back to our house. It showed up two days after our parents told us they were getting divorced. I remember coming downstairs and all of us sitting at the kitchen table. I think I remember Neil crying. For years I dreamed that after Mom and Dad told us, all four of us ran from the room at once, bolting like startled animals. I remember the dream more than what really happened.

But my sharpest memory from that week is walking home from school the day the toys arrived. Neil's with me and we're quiet, just walking, but then he says, "Mom's going to move to San Francisco."

"How do you know?"

"She told me. For work, she said. That's where all her clients are."

I try to imagine my mom making a new life in a city I've never been to, far away from our house, our driveway, our kitchen and its familiar smells. I think about it the way I pick at scabs.

Then Neil and I turn the corner into our cul-de-sac and there they are in our driveway: two wooden crates bigger than our dad's car, resting on pallets, shipped from Los Angeles, California. Two crates full of my winnings, the toys I had grabbed, the things that would save me.

Preeti Vangani

Textbook & Desire

At school I study the female anatomy: uterus, fundus, ovary, and cervix.
At home I help my sister look for parts missing from her doll

while the actress on TV sings *Sone sone patole lakhan. There are millions
of beautiful girls.* She is an item-song girl. An item-song is a fantasy,

a relief, a release, unconnected to the narrative of the film. Plugged
in to titillate more people to come to the screens. She lies semi-naked

in a bathtub covering her nipples like eyes being shut for hide-and-seek.
Our eyes become detectives, peer into an opening under the settee.

Our hands broom the floor for the feel of plastic. A hundred male hands
in black gloves are superimposed on the item girl as she wiggles waist
   down.

The chorus comes on. We dismiss our search, mirror her dance moves.
But I am the only golden baby doll, we chime, we shimmy our shoulders.

She seems ecstatic. The song ends. The item-girl doesn't return.
She isn't plot or plot point. We drop Knockoff Barbie in the storeroom.

in a box filled with items that need to be sorted into trash or charity.

Allyson Young

Nell as Cat Ballou

Sometimes, in my head, it's Nell, but sometimes it's Cat Ballou,
sometimes, zipped up tight in a chili-hot dress, leaning real sexy
against the doorframe of the cheesy set of a dirty train car & she's
saying
eat it baby, & *get it down quick,*
this new stuff,
our full
fluctuation.

Like a girl in a cheap movie, I follow her, slowly,
all that wood-paneling, that dark, dark, car.

        ...

> & then the light changes suddenly & I'm eighteen, here, in
> black lacquer pants, but also I'm ten in new school shoes
> & I'm four in tangerine stripes & mostly I am missing my
> mother & really, this is a feeling which, like most of my
> feelings, like sadness, is a little like a full balloon & like me
> & is about to burst.

Allyson Young

Nell at Girl Scout Camp

Nell & I are drifting to sleep one night, when we hear a knocking against the rocks by our tent's door. A mink. Dark-cloud-lightning. Two voices, tied in a knot around a sugar maple tree. We scream & run through the thick woods. Pine trees the color of eyelids. Or penny-rust-green. We get caught in the thorns of a thick rosebush & we keep running. We reach the great room—the dust & the stuffed moose. We hide from the boys in us in the fireplace. We compare the shapes of our injuries.

M. Brett Gaffney

Blood

One fall I worked two jobs:
doggie daycare and haunted house.

And when I came home, bitten
and monstered, he asked me

if all the blood was mine.
Now, I pull on stained jeans,

one knee torn up like country back road.
Not all the blood is real.

But it feels like armor just the same,
true final-girl fashion.

The denim hugs my body,
remembering its hurt and hum,

the way I painted wounds on my skin,
pretending for a night

that I knew how much blood,
how many sharp teeth,

it would take to turn me
into something brave.

Whitney Collins

The Nest

On Tuesday, Frankie's father took her two places against his will. The first was to see her premature brothers at Our Lady of Peace NICU. Three days prior, and sixty days too early, James and Jasper had slipped out of Frankie's mother like a pair of feeble insects that doctors promptly secured under glass for observation both scientific and sacred. In the ensuing emergency, Frankie's father, unable to locate a sitter, deposited his six-year-old daughter on the foot of his blind mother's nursing-home bed with a naked baby doll and a box of Sun-Maid raisins.

For two days, Frankie watched *The Young and the Restless* and *Who Wants to Be a Millionaire* from a vinyl recliner, eating saltines and applesauce and drinking Boost, while her grandmother's friends leaned on walkers in the doorway, admiring her like a misplaced peacock. "She's a prodigy," the grandmother claimed. "She's in first grade and can balance a checkbook. She knows all the Canadian provinces."

Every so often, the grandmother would run her fingers over Frankie's soft face as if her eyebrows were made of Braille and tell her the baby brothers would probably die. "They're like worms on a summer sidewalk, child. They don't stand a chance in the dry heat of this world." To Frankie, this honestly felt so much like affection that sometimes she asked her grandmother to repeat herself, which the grandmother did with gusto, adding details about Frankie's father and her Uncle Eric. How they weren't born early, but they'd been stuck together at the hip and the doctors had to slice the grandmother open to remove them. "I was the one who almost died," she said. "Those boys were laying inside me, side by side, like a butterfly. Your father. He got the hip. Eric, he never was right." At this, the grandmother

---

patted Frankie's face and body with her hands. "Looks like you'll make it," she said, smiling. "You're one of the lucky ones." Then Frankie, full of herself, excused herself to faux tap-dance in the hallway for nickels, making four dollars in one commercial break—enough to buy just one brother something in the hospital gift shop.

Back in the recliner, Frankie covered herself with an afghan that smelled of menthol. She saw that her grandmother was on the verge of sleep, so she asked, "Did it hurt when they pulled the babies out of you?"

Her grandmother jolted, frowned, then nodded. "It was hell," she quietly moaned. "Oh, child. Let me tell you: I know hell."

Frankie thought about this in the dark while the mute television featured a brown man selling electric grills that nothing stuck to, not even cheese. Frankie knew a little about hell. About how, in October, she'd turn seven. How then she'd be considered responsible for everything she did and everything she thought. How the week before Halloween, Father Greg would be waiting for her and her classmates in the church booth to tell him everything they had ever done wrong.

Frankie had already started the list in her mind. She had stolen a pack of Juicy Fruit from the drugstore when she was four. She had dropped one of her mother's diamond earrings down the drain (on accident) and never told (on purpose) when she was five. And once, just a month ago, when her mother was too pregnant to get off the park bench, Frankie had come across a boy inside the playground tunnel beating a rock against a limp chipmunk. When he offered her a turn, she said OK but made the mistake of wrapping her hand completely around the rock so that when she hit the chipmunk, her knuckles could feel its bones break, could feel how it was still warm. Frankie had decided to only mention the gum to Father Greg, which would be another sin. The more Frankie thought about it, the more she couldn't see a way to keep herself out of hell. But she fell asleep, regardless.

On Tuesday, the nursing home manager came to the grandmother's room. He stood in the doorway and explained that Frankie, by law, had to leave. Frankie gathered up her things but not before noticing that the toes of the man's shoes were wrapped in black tape to hold the soles on. In his office, he called her father and said, "Either you or the police can come pick her up."

☾

33

Last November, to everyone's surprise, Uncle Eric called to invite Frankie and her parents to Thanksgiving dinner at his house.

"He says your mother will be there with her nurse," Frankie's mother said to Frankie's father. "Maybe he's finally trying."

"Right," her father said. "Don't hold your breath."

On the day of the party, Frankie's mother dressed Frankie in a brown sashed dress and a gray wool coat with brass buttons. Frankie had only met her uncle once before, at her grandfather's funeral. She remembered he'd stood under a pine tree away from the crowd, holding an umbrella even though it wasn't raining.

"Will any kids be there?" Frankie asked.

"No," her mother said. "Just you."

When they arrived at his house, Frankie covered her mouth to hide her joy. The bungalow was painted bright purple with an orange front door, and on the roof, attached to the chimney with duct tape, was a faded, plastic Santa Claus.

"Jesus," her father sighed.

"David," her mother said.

For dinner, instead of turkey and stuffing and a normal-sized pumpkin pie that fed eight people, Eric served each guest a tiny, roasted quail and minuscule mounds of sweet potatoes scooped with a melon baller and dwarfed apple tarts the size of poker chips. In her whole young life, Frankie had never been so delighted. There were ropes of blue tinsel over every doorway and glitter sprinkled on the tablecloth and six strangers at the meal that were of no relation to Frankie or her parents or her blind grandmother but who loved on Frankie more than she'd ever been loved on before—strangers who looked like women but talked like men and smoked cigarettes as long as chopsticks and cried every time a song came on the radio.

"The dishes," Eric announced at dinner, pinching up a teacup for everyone to see, "are antique doll's china from Russia."

Frankie inspected her plate with awe. The dinner guests, the ones who weren't family, gasped.

"They belonged to Anna Rasputin," Uncle Eric said. "Anna Goddamned Rasputin. That's how much I love you all."

Frankie ate four apple tarts and eleven scoops of sweet potatoes. Her quail was so precious she wrapped it in her napkin then excused herself to the bathroom. She found her winter coat in the hallway and placed the bird in its inner silk pocket.

Frankie noticed her father did not eat. Frankie noticed her grandmother's nurse, Concetta, excused the grandmother from the dining table and fed her from a paper plate in the living room. Frankie noticed her mother spent the whole meal watching Frankie's father in the same way she watched Frankie when she ran a fever. Frankie noticed Uncle Eric noticed none of this.

After dinner, Uncle Eric took Frankie upstairs to his bedroom, where he showed her a red toy piano. "We must bring this downstairs," he said, flushed and wide-eyed. "We've got to keep the teeny, tiny theme going." Frankie nodded in agreement. "What do you play, Frankie? 'Für Elise'? Please tell me you play 'Für Elise'."

Frankie was worried; she only knew "The Indian Song." "I only know 'The Indian Song'," she said.

"That's perfect!" Uncle Eric said, placing the piano on the shoulder opposite his cane. "Because guess who invented Thanksgiving, Sugar?" Frankie shrugged. "The motherfucking Indians, that's who."

On their way downstairs with the piano, Frankie and Uncle Eric met Frankie's father on his way upstairs. "It's time to go, Frankie. Your mother is waiting on the porch."

Uncle Eric stomped a foot. "You're leaving?" he huffed. "But Frankie was just going to play us a song."

Frankie's father shook his head. "Frankie will not be participating in your circus, Eric."

"Circus?" Uncle Eric exclaimed. "That's what you call this?" Uncle Eric waved his cane in all directions. "I spent six days getting this ready. Do you know how hard it was to find twelve quail that would fit on that china? I took one of Anna Rasputin's doll plates around to four butchers and then a farm. Four butchers and a farm, David."

Frankie stood and watched. Uncle Eric's blue eyelids looked heavy. Her father had his feet on two different steps, as if he might pounce. "Why can't you just do things the regular way?" her father said. "Why couldn't there have been a normal turkey? And why all these people, Eric? Answer me that." Uncle Eric patted his pockets with the crook of his cane. Frankie knew he was looking for a cigarette. "I'll tell you why," her father continued. "It's because it's never about anybody but you. It's about what you want. It's about drawing attention to yourself. It's not about Thanksgiving or family. It's about Eric. The Eric Show."

Frankie looked at her uncle. She wondered what he might say. How he might make her father feel terrible for what he'd just done.

But Uncle Eric said nothing. He simply lifted the toy piano off his shoulder and into the air with one hand and then threw the piano down the stairs, over Frankie's father's head and onto the first-floor landing, where it jangled and splintered in a way that almost made Frankie laugh. It was exciting to see her father scared, even for a flash. Frankie's father reached up and yanked her down by her dress sash to the step his back foot was on. Uncle Eric pulled out a pack of Viceroys and pointed at his brother. "Get the fuck out," he said. "And, Frankie? I love you."

On the ride home, Frankie's mother and father were silent. Neither of them moved—not one millimeter. It was as if the car drove itself. In the back seat, Frankie sat, replaying the piano scene. Up it went, her father cringed, down it came, exploding in a plinking pile. Frankie smiled wide in the dark in her brass-buttoned coat. She placed her hand over the lump that was the hidden quail.

When Frankie's mother saw her in the doorway of her hospital room, she succumbed to a spasm of sobs that Frankie at first mistook for uncontrollable laughter and that her father, quite clearly, had grown accustomed to. Maybe even tired of.

"You remember Frankie, Catherine," her father said as if reintroducing them at a dinner party. "She's come to see her brothers."

Frankie's mother convulsed in the wheelchair on the way to the NICU. "They're …," she struggled, "so tiny, Frankie. Say a prayer," she choked. "Oh, God. Say your prayers."

Frankie was revulsed by her mother's brokenness, by her desperate pleas for the pointless type of prayers that had no beginning or end. She touched her mother's hair absentmindedly to pretend she was not appalled, but her curiosity over James and Jasper outweighed her compassion, and she tried to make up for this by showing her mother the fringe of her socks. Frankie did not like fringed socks, but her grandmother had insisted she dress as if for a recital. On Monday, her grandmother had sent a nurse out to buy a pair of patent leather shoes and dress socks on her lunch break, and Frankie had been instructed to go to the grandmother's jewelry box and give the nurse a gold watch for her efforts.

"See my socks?" Frankie said, smiling, looking past her mother's contorted face. "See my shoes?" *Where were these brothers?* was what Frankie really wondered. *How terrifying would they be?*

To Frankie's delight, they were horrendous. Beetles under bell jars. Featherless starlings fallen from a nest. Their skin red and shiny, their matchstick arms like roasted chicken wings stretched out to reveal pitiful armpits, their closed eyes bulbous and alien. Nurses turned them this way and that way with green latex gloves, adjusting the tape and tubes and gaping diapers, but nothing made them look better or better off. When Frankie watched them, she imagined all the times she had twisted a coin in a candy machine only to forget to cup her hands under the silver spout. She remembered all the times a gumball had escaped her, rolling under the desk at a carwash or on the tarry carpet of a Mexican restaurant. All the times she had been forced to beg for a second quarter. And now, see? Her mother would have to ask for two. Frankie watched her brothers breathe, their tiny ribcages pumping to the beat of a frantic song. *Scary, scary, scary. Very, very, very.* Frankie could tell one of them was worse off than the other—Jasper, it seemed, from the sign on his little greenhouse. Frankie decided to root for him. *Go, Jasper,* she thought. *Beat James.* She knew this was terrible and she bent down to check that the lace of her socks was still folded neatly.

"I know it's hard to believe," her father said unconvincingly. "But one day your brothers will grow up to be big and strong. Bigger and stronger than you."

Frankie was done looking at them. She tapped her new shoes against the tile floor of the hospital hallway to show her parents she was the same she had always been. "Can I go to the gift shop?" Frankie asked. "I have four dollars."

Her father nodded, and after they wheeled Frankie's mother back to her room, downstairs, in the hospital store, Frankie bought a tiny, blue T-shirt that said *Early Bird.*

"Who's that for?" her father asked.

Frankie put it on her naked doll as they walked to the car in the heavy August heat. *Go, Jasper,* she thought. *Beat James.* "It's for my baby," she said.

The second place Frankie's father took her that day against his will was to his brother's, back to the Thanksgiving neighborhood where rainbow windsocks blew horizontal from porches.

"If I had my way …," her father began as he searched for a parking spot.

"You'd rather take me to the zoo," Frankie finished for him. "Why don't you go back to the hospital?" She changed the subject. "Before something bad happens."

Frankie's father slouched at the wheel, and she felt a small surge of victory in her stomach. "You can just drop me off," she said. "I know which house is his."

But her father parked and walked her up the stairs to the purple bungalow, where Uncle Eric met them on the porch. He wore a silk bathrobe and a pair of red, velvet slippers. He held an unlit cigarette and a new, jaunty magician's cane in one hand and placed his other hand on top of Frankie's head. "We're going to have a big time," he said. "You and me, sugar. A grand old time."

Frankie left the men on the porch and went inside to snoop. She overheard her father say, low and tense, "Don't pull any of your shit."

In Uncle Eric's living room, Frankie watched a working stoplight in the corner cycle through its red-yellow-green. In his downstairs bathroom, she saw that the toilet water was blue. She flushed it once to see if it was blue again and it was and she was thrilled. In the kitchen, in the refrigerator, Frankie found a pink cake with one slice missing. "Happy Tuesday —itch," Frankie said aloud with her hands on her hips.

"I ate the W," Uncle Eric confessed from the doorway. "And it was delicious."

Frankie turned. She suddenly felt shy but refused to show it. "My brothers will probably die," she said. "They're like two worms on a summer sidewalk. They don't stand a chance in the dry heat of this world."

Uncle Eric snorted, shocked. "Gurrrrrl," he purred, fumbling through the pocket of his robe. "Go on, now. Tell us how you really feel." He produced a lighter and lit his cigarette and looked hard into Frankie's eyes when he exhaled.

"It's true," she said. "I've seen them. They're probably dead right now."

Uncle Eric shook his head admiringly. "I doubt that, hon. What with modern medicine and all. But still." He shuffled to the refrigerator with his cane and brought out the cake, from which he cut a slice and served to Frankie on a paper towel at the chrome table. "I bet they looked bad off." He sat down across from Frankie with an amber ashtray and a coffee mug shaped like a woman's breast. "Didn't anybody tell you the story of your dad's and my birth? Everybody thought we wouldn't make it. And now, see? Look." Uncle Eric tilted his head back like a supermodel and puckered his lips. He rapped his cane on the floor three times. "They were right about one of us." At this, Eric laughed long and hard, and Frankie could tell he expected her to do the same. Eric pointed to her cake and then at her. "Oh, I'm just playing, doll." He crushed out his cigarette and winked. "Now, you eat that, and then I want to show you something."

In the grandmother's jewelry box, next to the gold watch, Frankie had found a tarnished silver locket, as dark as if it had been dropped into a fire, as black as the lung the doctor had held up on television to warn children against smoking. Inside the locket, on the right side, was a small, round picture of Frankie's father when he was about her age, which Frankie could not imagine had ever been the case, but there it was: photographic proof. On the left side of the locket, there was a tiny dot of glue and a white flake of photo paper. Uncle Eric was missing, having fallen off, Frankie guessed, after years of having a blind woman rake her hands over him. But as her grandmother dozed and Frankie messed through the giant, synthetic pearls and tangles of brassy chains, Uncle Eric's round face appeared, ghostly, inside a tiny cellophane envelope, an insect's wing among scrap metal. From what Frankie could gather, Uncle Eric had been removed and relocated with intention, plucked off by her grandmother's thick, clouded fingernails.

Frankie thought of this as Uncle Eric brought out his dress. It was a floor-length gown with a mermaid cut, made of thousands of red feathers. On his shoulders he wore a sequined red, blue, and yellow cape that he could slide his arms into and spread like wings. "I'm a scarlet macaw," he said. "I'm thinking I should make a hood for it. To go over my head. With a beak and all."

Frankie was mesmerized. Her grandmother had most certainly removed the wrong picture. "What's it for?" she asked her uncle in a voice cleaned of disinterest. "Where will you wear it?"

Eric leaned on his cane. "My show, sugar," he said. "I wear it and I sing the song 'Somebody, Somewhere' by Loretta Lynn. You know Loretta, sweetheart?"

Frankie shook her head. She wasn't interested in the song part. "Where's your nest?" she asked. "Every bird needs a nest."

Eric stopped and said nothing. He was thinking. "A nest," he whispered, his eyes darting around the room as if collecting supplies. "You mean, like an origin story?"

"No," Frankie said. "Like a nest."

Uncle Eric leaned forward on his cane, his long fingers curled over the crook like a parrot grasping its perch. "You want to know where I came from? I dream it all the time. I've had the same dream for thirty-eight years."

Frankie thought of her grandmother. "Your mother?"

Eric rolled his eyes. "Oh, sister, please. Air France. I have this dream I'm on an Air France plane. Except it's not so much a plane as it is a saucer. It's like an Air France UFO. And I'm flying on it with hundreds and hundreds of other people. At this point, I've had the dream so many times, I've started to recognize these people. To anticipate them. They're decent, I guess. But I can't find any common denominator. We're not all trannies. We're not all Americans. But there we are: on an Air France UFO flying from Charles de Gaulle to fucking—sorry, freaking—Atlanta."

Frankie frowned. "That's how you got here?"

Eric nodded, fumbling through his robe pockets for his lighter and Viceroys. "Yep." He produced a cigarette, which seemed to bring him the same sort of relief Frankie'd felt when her father had said it was time to leave the hospital. "So," said Eric. "Where did you come from?"

Frankie thought for a moment. "My parents went down to the train station and showed the conductor a ticket. Like the kind you show the butcher when you wait in line for a roast."

Eric exhaled rapidly in approval. "And?"

"He gave them a suitcase and I was in it." Frankie thought some more. "I looked pretty good to them until a few years later. That was when they started going down to the train station for another baby, but the suitcases they kept picking up were empty. Then I didn't look so great anymore. I was like when you look at a word for a really long time and it stops making sense."

"Oh, this is good, doll baby."

"And they just kept going down to the train station with their butcher ticket until finally the conductor got tired of them, and to make them go away he gave them a suitcase out of the lost-and-found." Frankie folded her arms and shook her head as if she stood on the sidelines of a playing field, spectating a losing team. "The suitcase had two babies in it, but they'd been in lost-and-found for a long time and didn't look so good."

Uncle Eric looked like he was going to cry. "Oh, princess," he sniffed. "You're an old soul, you know that?"

Frankie thought for a moment. Uncle Eric smoked and flapped his cape. "Where do you think babies go when they die? Back to the train station?"

Uncle Eric sat on the edge of his bed. He tapped his cigarette out on the bottom of his slipper, and Frankie watched the red embers fall to the braided rug and die. Then he lit a second cigarette and Frankie thought of his lungs, a black, tarnished locket open in his chest. "I don't know where babies go when they die," he said. "I don't know where grown-ups go."

Frankie stood and assessed Uncle Eric's bedroom. She began with a quilt, which she placed in the center of the round, braided rug, and she made it into the base of a nest. Then she went looking for other things in his drawers and closet: a towel, a second silk robe, a set of paisley sheets. "In October I have my First Reconciliation," she said. "I have to tell Father Greg all the things I've ever done wrong. Then in April I take Communion. That means from then on, if I die, I go to hell if I'm not sorry."

Eric exhaled and shook his head and rapped out his second cigarette on his slipper with such intent that Frankie thought the rug or his shoe might catch on fire. "Oh, Jesus H. Christ," he said. "No seven-year-old is going to hell."

Frankie shrugged. "It wouldn't scare me," she said. "I might even like it."

Uncle Eric bowed his head. "You and me both. I wouldn't know a damn soul in heaven, anyway." He reached out to hug Frankie and she let him, but she kept her arms at her side. She wanted to hug him back, but then when her father came to take her home, she'd be devastated—all hollowed out.

"Let's make the nest," she said.

"Yes," Uncle Eric said, clapping his hands together once. "Let's."

Frankie and Uncle Eric gathered all the clothes and towels and bedding they could find in his room. There were velvets and terry-cloths, batiks and patchworks, paisleys and polka dots and shawls with knotted fringe. When they were done, they sat in the middle of it and each ate a slice of pink cake.

"You didn't eat a W," Frankie said. "You ate a B."

Uncle Eric's eyes turned big and bright. "There's no fooling you, sister. What else do you know?"

Frankie licked icing from her fingertips. "I know my mother will never be the same. I know my father wants to run away. I know I'll lie to Father Greg." Frankie began to wrap a long scarf around her baby doll. She started with its feet and wound the scarf around its body until it was a tight, lavender cocoon. She handed it to Uncle Eric. "And I know I want Jasper to make it, but he won't, and that James will be the one who lives instead. And I already don't like James because he's the reason Jasper won't live."

Uncle Eric was as quiet as Frankie could imagine a person being. She looked at his long eyelashes, at the way his lips seemed stained with wine, his eyelids stained with ink. She watched his slender hands, how his fingernails were all different lengths, some as short as a construction worker's, some as long as Miss America's. She watched as he wrapped the baby doll in a second scarf. Then he handed it to Frankie and she wrapped it in a third. Then she handed it back to him for a fourth. They went on like this, silent, back and forth with the doll, until it was dark outside and the cicadas were as loud as a thousand wire brushes on drumskins and the baby doll was the size of a Virginia ham and they set it in the nest like an egg and went to bed in the guest room, where there were still some blankets.

"So, you don't know Loretta?" Uncle Eric asked in the dark. Frankie shook her head on the pillow. "She was born in Butcher Hollow, right here in Kentucky, and she had three sisters and four brothers, and she got married when she was fifteen."

Frankie was thinking of her patent-leather shoes. She was thinking of the box they came in. She kept seeing Jasper in the box. She kept trying, in her mind, to cover him up with tissue paper, but the tissue paper kept sliding off.

"She's had sixteen number-one songs." Uncle Eric lit a cigarette as they lay in bed. It crackled red in the dark, then he exhaled. "Somebody, somewhere, don't know what he's missin' tonight," he began to sing, in a way that almost sounded like talking. "Lord, here sits a woman, just lonesome enough to be right. For love 'em or leave 'em, how I need someone to hold tight."

In her mind, Frankie was able to pull the tissue paper completely over Jasper. But through it, she could still see his face. Like Uncle Eric's in the cellophane envelope.

Uncle Eric gave a little laugh from his side of the bed. "Oh, sugar," he said. "I can't sing worth shit. But I sure have had a nice time with you."

Frankie pretended to be asleep. Downstairs, she could hear the click of Uncle Eric's stoplight as it cycled through its colors. She knew you couldn't hear that click in the real world. No one out there knew stoplights made any sound at all.

In the morning, Frankie woke to the sound of crying. It was Uncle Eric, back in his bedroom, sitting at the window with the last piece of cake, looking out at a gray, windless day.

Frankie came and stood at his side. She could see the windsocks drooped from the trees like real socks. "Which one was it?" she asked.

Water ran from Uncle Eric's eyes. Not from one corner or another but from the entire eye. "The little one," he whispered. "He never stood a chance."

Frankie thought of her ruined parents. She thought of James at the age of nine, fat, in a baseball dugout. She thought of Uncle Eric's hip, how the bones were like two puzzle pieces that didn't fit but how doctors had pushed on them anyway to make it look like they had finished something. And Frankie thought of her gray, wool coat with the brass buttons. How it had been hanging in the back of her bedroom closet since Thanksgiving. How, in its inner, silk pocket, still wrapped in one of Uncle Eric's napkins, was the quail.

Michelle Donahue

Feeding Crows

A little girl feeds crows, lets loose
peanuts, dog food, leftovers,
to scatter the browning grass
with those dark-feathered bodies.

And in return? The crows
come with small favors, metallic
bolts, a single earring, a small light
bulb unscrewed and abandoned.

We always come with something;
we do not expect free gifts. The girl
loves the birds' angular wings, how
food lures beaks and bodies, black
splashed like oil, like ink.

But I've seen crows drop nuts
in intersections, lure other birds
to that temporarily empty space,
until the light turns green
and bird skulls meet bumpers.

The crows wait for that red turn:
our metallic lights that indicate
safety. The crows retrieve those
smashed bodies, nature's impulse,
to take all it can get.

From impulsive hands, the girl feeds crows.
How simple they are, how trusting

Dakota Canon

All the Missing Children

They find their way when the sky
is black. They don't need maps

or GPS. Some think it's melody
that leads them, or the bright colors

of wildflowers, like beacons in the
night. They bring washup bags,

toothbrushes and Vapor Rub,
and choose twisted branches

to untwist and climb. The meadow grasses
fold when they jump and run,

and everyone trembles when they're caught.
In the gathering house that smells

musty from rotting wood, they compose
harmonies, write lyrics to the piper's

songs and drink hot chocolate
spiced with rum. When someone cries,

the others don't point or laugh, because
the mountains are high on all sides, and

bullet holes are in fashion.

Hussain Ahmed

Shadows

Dapchi 2018

the window creaks were dirges   swallowed
in the rays that dried out the blood on my skin.
I have seen stars fall, but I don't know how the ashes look.
in the back yard, my hen had hatched all its eggs
and I noticed   there were too many hawks on the sky today—
maybe they had been all along.
the hen opened my eyes to what had been obviously invisible.
the men that defined entropy tell of the chaos in a room
full of girls in their hundreds, dragged through a field of stones.
entropy is the degree of randomness that comes with being scared
of how you look in the mirror   after gulping too much water.
the mirror on our bathroom wall is a sheet of foil
clustered with many shadows, it shimmers only when it rains.
the girls try so hard to remember their old names.
they again thought of home   the windows they jumped
and the guns that spoke the language they had known all their lives.
I want to stop writing about the blood on the walls   but I have the moon
in my front pocket,   it's so easy to locate me on the map.
when everywhere turns dark   I embrace all I could not see
and assume *oblong* to be the shape of the world   when Dapchi was
   raided
Wikipedia claimed their history only began when their daughters were
   kidnapped,
because that night, even the crickets did not forgo their songs.

Jim Daniels

Pinned

Fifteen seconds. Not even enough for a good apology.
Fifteen seconds. Enough to pin a young man flat
        to the padded mat.
Fifteen seconds. Long enough to type those two
        words.
Fifteen seconds. Long enough to kill a man
        with your braggart's gun.
Fifteen seconds. All it took for me to cradle you,
        shoulders flat to the mat,
                the coach slapping palm against it.
Fifteen seconds. You'll be late for class, young
        man, late slip, detention, life in prison.
Fifteen seconds. Tired of hearing it?
Fifteen seconds. Your mother not making you
        any more PB and J's, her neat diagonal slice.
Fifteen seconds, long enough to identify
        a bad song and switch the station, driving
        around with a body in the trunk.
Fifteen seconds. Long enough to flunk the test
        when you have not read a word.
Fifteen seconds. Long enough to count the money
        and know you've been ripped off.
Fifteen seconds of shame, thirty seconds
        of fame, ticking backward into the lower
        left corner of the newspaper. Body found.
        Snow bank at the junior high. Why practice
        if you're not going to fire? No blanks
        in the basement, nobody home to hear

---

the makeshift shooting range,
to wonder at the shredded mattress
slumped against a wall.
Fifteen seconds. Remember me? I hope
not, pinning you, crossing your name
off the tournament bracket on the gym wall.
Fifteen seconds of triumph followed by the lack
of referees forever after. *I'll kill you,*
you said. Both of us the same weight, fair for
fifteen seconds. What made you tough, living
in an identical house, four blocks over?
Stealing money from hallway
wimps and bathroom fools.
Fifteen seconds of the coach's grin. *Not so tough,*
are you? Hey, killer, I remember you.
No need to type your name.

Dustin M. Hoffman

The Life Net

Because who else will catch you when you must jump, when there's no other path but plummet? Because when you're quaking from your third-floor window, smoke blackening your vision, flames singing skin, we are salvation. Because is why we exist. We are the beaming, white circle in darkness, the red bullseye. We, the fine firefighters of this great blistering nation, will catch you in our life net. So jump unto us.

Or, first, watch as we demonstrate the miracle. We swivel from half-moon storage position to locked life-saving circle in seconds. This is how we've rescued for a century, since Thomas F. Browder, our inventor, first rustled from epiphanous dreams to scribble circumferences and springs on the plaster wall beside his bed, since his ingenious patent in 1887. We stow Browder's likeness in lockets against our chests, tap them and pray to our saint of ingenuity, always ask what Browder would do, because Browder knows best. You may be thinking—you up there on the roof with your arms crossed over your chest and your pursed lips and your pissy posture and your cordless phone and your blissfully cruel certainty in our obsolescence—that we are superstitious relics, that we are clowns clinging to a trampoline. It is not a trampoline. We disdain that conflation. We say "life net" or "safety sheet" because we are not children playing with toys. We are men—and one woman—saving lives.

The one being Gertie. Just watch her and us grip the metal frame, huddle shoulder-to-shoulder, shuffle across the sidewalk in perfect synchronicity. You smirk at our ballet, scoff at the beauty of grace under crushing pressure. You shake your head at our chorus of grunts, and we forgive you your cynicism. Suit yourself, spectating from the roof of the town's tallest building. We'll be back for you when you're ready.

Watch: a woman, a mother, shins stretched over the windowsill, sooty tangles flouncing over her eyes. Look more closely at what she proffers in her outstretched hands: a baby, a child, can't be more than one year old, complete innocence. The child does not squirm. Stoic calmness soothes their limp limbs. The child is not dead but curious, as you should be if you'd stop trying to dial an operator from the rooftop and allow yourself admiration and just witness. We are the first and only responders, your only response to rooftop desertion.

The mother's hands part and the child is baptized by floating, freefalling from fire and smoke and collapse. This child-turned-angel. We raise our arms, hoist the life net's frame. At the instant of impact, the moment bare thighs meet safety sheet, we drop so sweetly, become pillow, feather, perfection together. Then we tilt one side and the infant rolls into Rolland's arms. The child does not cry, is preoccupied plucking at Rolland's fine auburn whiskers.

We forgot the mother, you narrate into your Camcorder. You aim the lens at her, zoom in, click the back of your throat, assume we can't handle a third-floor adult. Which would then mean that you, all the way up there, are hopeless. Fear not. Behold. She takes coaxing, and Seamus is our golden boy with big green eyes and perfect teeth, and he convinces her to fly through a series of waving arms and throaty murmurs. Her skirt billows in the air, and we glance only to gauge descent, never to notice the white panties with the tear against the right buttock. We catch and she's safe in Rolland's arms then reunited with child—a Madonna glowing atop Browder's miraculous arc of saving.

Yes, watch as we don't linger for the crowds to flash their Polaroids and Instamatics. If you won't abandon your electronic marvels and jump now, then we're off. And, so, we go deeper into the city, where ten-story buildings prick the skyline, where the FM radio towers needle at God. We eye black billows, smoldering roof tar, and treated lumber ablaze. Our hearts thrill, yet we won't crack smiles. That would be insensitive. That would be betrayal. We must hate the fire we love to best. We must hurry somberly, the precious lift net folded and hoisted across our shoulders.

The burning culprit stretches high, and we exhale a secret sigh that there are only eight stories to this apartment complex. Any higher and the life net flirts with failure. Flames spout out some windows. Out others, survivors flap yellowed blankets. There are dozens trapped, to which Browder will deliver salvation. We snap open the life net and huddle into position. The low floors first, where we are confident in spring support, in the alloy-wire mesh's tensile strength. We catch three children, two men, four mothers, one senior with hair the color of ladder rungs, two cats, two dogs, and one boa constrictor that coils into a question mark around the bullseye. Our biceps and forearms ache with success. Our thighs throb, and Elmer's bad knees are getting worse, but adrenal pride remedies all. We will not be stopped.

One final cry stings the air. An ancient man bellows from the seventh floor, yelling through his naked gums, orange flames reflected in his bare scalp. He may only have a handful of months left, but he shrieks and flails to keep them. With his leopard-print liver spots, he certainly doesn't create a photo opportunity, wouldn't be fit for the newspaper front page that we wouldn't smile for anyway. We don't rescue for fleeting glamour.

We hup-hup-hup in formation to his window and spread the net. We worry about soft bones, but you and he and we must remember that all we can offer is a chance, a better option than burning. So we plead for this curmudgeonly hermit to make haste into gravity's grip.

He ducks back inside smoke. After too many scalding seconds pass, he pops his silver beard out the window. His arms hug a stack of books. He rains leather-bound Mellvilles and first-edition Cathers. Their golden typefaces shimmer, but their beauty means nothing to Browder, nothing compared to even a single threadbare life. We flap their splayed pages onto the sidewalk and shout for him to jump. He's busy, though, pelting the bullseye with copper statues, pewter paperweights, silver medallions. Then lithographs and lamps and cigar boxes and silk robes and knobby, bronze doorknobs hail downward. This exhibit of curios ricochets into our chests and faces. We turn our heads, lose our rhythm, and this must be why we miss the ancient hoarder's jump.

His drop yanks our arms before we understand our catch, and then the storm is over. Nothing stirs. When we finally gather the courage to witness, we see that the man has landed atop his treasure. A bronze cowboy's arm pierces the man's esophagus. His neck whiskers gleam with ruby wetness. His spine zigs over hardbacks and sepia globes. Instead of seizing a final few nonagenarian months, instead of even a few more wheezing breaths of smoke, he has died in our net. The life net's canvas stains with his blood, the red bullseye now blurred into an amorphous oval.

But we don't have time for bleach or grief. There is work to do and we plunge into the city's tentacle streets. A ladder truck rockets past our foot-soldiering. The smoke it chases hasn't even crept into our nostrils, must be miles away, so we stalk the siren's echoes. If there's a chance to lend our hands, callused from the life net's metal frame, then we must persist. Into the sunset we march, trailing the last decibels of siren song.

Once the sun sets, the world seems on fire—one thousand lights spritzing halo-orange glow. Night and day blur behind electricity's bullying. Years could be passing while we wander and wonder, and we are tricked. Elmer tugs the life net right toward a blinking, neon-pink LIVE NUDES sign. Solly pulls left toward the simmering, red pawn-store promise: WE BUY GOLD. We lurch toward the fluorescent, plastic flames advertising a fast-food, flame-broiled burger. The customers gawk over suspended sandwiches while we stare through the window, stomachs growling and faces hot, life net at the ready. Rolland wonders if we better just give in and go home.

Then a glorious blazing appears. It alights the night sky. The town's tallest factory spits fire. Two ladder trucks are already on scene, cranked up through black clouds. We can't see our comrades working up there, through all that smoke, but we assume their greatness, tap our Browder lockets, and pray for the best, recite his patent: … *combine simplicity, strength, and efficiency, together with capabilities of being packed in a small compass.* We hope their usefulness will exist in perpetuity. Likewise, Browder's legacy must not be forgotten. The jump for one's life must remain an eternal human right.

The buildings have stacked so tall, we've lost ourselves in the city jungle. The towering either happened overnight or we've been fumbling through the city for years. We must admit how our heads dizzy gazing up at untested peaks. We scour the factory building's base, hunt survivors hanging out low-level windows. They have already evacuated. All that's left are the heights, and it hurts too deeply to admit inability. What choice do we really have? Do we dare depart from danger, from a single life that could be saved? We raise the life net, flash its bullseye and the ancient hermit's dried blood toward a fourteenth-floor man clad in a navy-blue uniform, stitched nametag winking from his heart. He seems unsure, takes something from his pocket, and a blue screen glows. And, so, we know it is you again, from your rooftop to this new height where you brandish your new gadgets that we don't understand, for which Browder didn't have time to amend his patents. What could you be doing with your pocketable screen instead of taking a chance at saving your life? The longer you tap and swipe and stare and plead into it, the farther the flames. The factory lengthens as we linger at the bottom, bolstered by Browder's brave spirit, yet you ignore us for that blue-glow sanctuary.

No more hesitation. Jump foolishly and fully. Release your tech and trust in straightforward mechanics, in simple physics, in one man's design of springs and metal and mesh and machine screws. You finally jump, and, true, we've never practiced a catch from this height, not even with the watermelons Sergio supplies from his garden and then pitches off the roof of town hall. Sergio's eyes flash the terror of uncertainty now, as all our eyes do. Our necks contort up at that smoke-laced sky, at your eternal descent. And we miss. Or you miss. Of course, all of us will miss at some point, even those gargantuan ladder trucks. There will never be enough of us to catch all who must jump. And Rolland is struck by falling limbs. He crumples.

We couldn't save you and your future-stuck dawdling, and now we bow around Rolland, check breathing, pulse, administer CPR, shout to the ladder trucks for whatever electrical marvels they've stashed inside their state-of-the-art metal beasts. But they don't hear us. They're too busy dragging ragdoll bodies down their ladders. There's not enough time, never enough. We kiss Rolland's hands, hug his neck. Another body crashes through the net while only half of us are still holding. This plummeting corpse is a blur ripping through the life net's fabric. We can't bear to examine the tear, the bone-blood slurry beneath our precious circle, can't bear to see Browder's patent shredded.

With clenched fists, we tug the fabric taut. Gertie heaves Rolland over her shoulder then onto the life net. We carry him away from a city grown too big for nets. We hustle like aimless animals. Our circle of saving is making circles, we realize, as we pass the blazing factory again. Or maybe this is a new fire. Or maybe every building burns.

Bodies tumble and streak and smack around us, aiming for our ruined net and Rolland's body. We dodge dozens. Hundreds. We are unable and ashamed and tuck our chins to whisper apology to Browder's locket likeness. How can any force prepare for the kind of explosion that is the city, the future, the corrupted cataclysm of knowing too much yet still unable to control a fire? Even Browder, that brilliant saint, never could've anticipated.

If we could, we'd raze every building down to six securable floors, maybe four, maybe just single stories too squat to ever pose a threat. We'd toss your glowing screens on the fire, stand too closely to watch while our own hair curled.

But not yet. Never yet. We have torn mesh and canvas to mend. We will take up needle and thread, sew like mad men and one mad woman. The work never stops. We will aim to be as excessive as water, as fire. Their spilling is endless, as ours will be. Because around this intersection, or maybe around this corner, we'll find our way out. There will be a cliff, a drop-off edge taller than any glass-skinned, steel-boned behemoth. Together, we'll jump that edge, lift Browder's life net above our heads, and float down toward safety.

BJ Love

The Question Then Is How to Love

anything without burning desire?
Without burning desire to the ground?
I don't mean devastation, but I do
mean ruin: the ruins of an old steel
factory, the ruins of Western expansion—
of the settlers who were actually more
unsettled, the ruins of an old church
where we're sure something of note
happened, we just weren't there
to write about it. My burning desire
has ruined everything I love, but
now that there are vines and flowers
growing over it, it feels purposeful
and worth revisiting like it never did
before. Like it's a past worth celebrating,
worth marking on my calendar. Last
weekend I watched two people get
married and I couldn't help but look
at my wife the whole time, wondering
at how, like the lone stone wall still
standing off in the distance, at how
we've ruined each other in the way
that is much more just nature taking
its toll. What I mean is that everything
costs us something, but if we let
the jasmine grow over us, we can
be beautiful, be delightful, forever.

Rachel Barton

A Time of Reckoning

From the third floor I see a woman run down the sidewalk
away from the hospital, her bathrobe flapping like wings.
Two cops dash after her. Later, a scrub jay sits in our hay-
colored grass with his back to me, his head tilted to one
side as he suns his wings to kill off the mites. A neighborhood cat approaches. You and I take the sofa bed, my husband
the mat on the floor, but then he joins us as an afterthought.
I move to the middle; you are slight as an elf, your narrow
back wingless. When you hear a wasp buzzing, you sit up to
study then lie back down. In the morning, something has
eaten one corner of the mattress, something with big teeth.

Cammy Thomas

Accounting

I found her old account book,
but it had no accounts,
just her journal on love,
her perfect round print,
meticulous line by line,

telling how love couldn't
be counted on except
to make her owe, how
she wished she could
hold him, how the sight of him
made her go weak.

This is my mother,
writing about our neighbor,
who taught her to fish.
His wife was her good friend
always, despite this feeling
that made my mother
faint. Only now and then
could they steal
a moment to yield.

We children suspected, felt
a change in the air when
she looked at him. But
she never said.

☾

What were those fishing trips like,
my mother with him and his wife,
the three of them hip deep
in the freezing river, creels
full of trout, and later
in the log cabin, mixing drinks?

Alyssa Proujansky

Pin a Person to the Earth

1.

A long time and a little time went by. The main characters were of a pale but ruddy countenance, like milk and blood. We were supposed to buy things with a minimal impact on aquatic life, but sometimes we did not. I dreamt of a ghost asking: *Do you really think this is the only place left to live?*

I saw a girl's hand, held, outstretched, to a wolf. I read about a rabbit, a three-legged cauldron, bright carrot stew. I heard about a wolf with his face made of rabbits, walking through a banquet hall.

Children sang a song about a feather bed: *It was made from the feathers of forty-leven geese, took a whole bolt of cloth for the tick!*

They shouted the word SCRAM.

Little cartoon animals cried, *Oh dear! Oh dear!*

A hawk soared, screeching, clawing its way through the blacky-blue night sky.

I drew the moon: in a jar, in a box. I felt arrows leave and enter my skin. I dreamt of a boy standing alone at the top of a hill, one paint-white blot of a star.

2.

I talked about interspaces and portals, the underworld. You talked about eclipses, pulses, trines, supermoons, water signs. I talked about your belt that was a vortex that was a belt—and took it off of you. I took my clothes off, too.

It was 10:10, 11:11. Clouds went by in stripes. I ate something, just to take its color into myself. Bright blots of berries stained the floor, behind the triple-locked doors of an office room. Two people who had only just recently met lay on a sheet, tracing dot-to-dot drawings on each other's bodies.

It is 12:34, you said, *and everything is as it is, is as it is supposed to be.*

3.

We had the same fever dream as children: infinity like an endless rectangle pressing in from all sides. I made hearts out of construction paper and pinned one to your chest. Sharp stars were embedded in my stomach, like glass contained in metal. I felt lines of anxiety, like walking into a tiny, fanged sea.

4.

I told you about the woman I'd loved: how she appeared in dreams, in classrooms and passages, in between, in the search for the middle.

Your laugher sounded wholesome—a wooden table in the afternoon; good, brown bread. I thought you were innocent in a way I was not.

5.

I made up stories about ghosts to get some distance: their runes and ruins, their workhouses and orphanages, their hieroglyphs and mines, their hobo signs.

We decided that ghosts try, but fail, to speak in: argot, shibboleth, béarlachas, rövarspråket, dulcarnon, pidgin.

That they suffer from the knowledge though not the symptoms of: consumption, botulism, boredom, fanaticism, trench mouth, plague, ague, water on the knee, hoof-and-mouth disease, ptomaine poisoning, ignorance, arrogance, the lines of the space between us.

I listed for you what ghosts cannot see: spiderwebs, glass jars, samovars, astrocytic endfeet, blood-brain barrier, horizon, human bodies and the ways they connect.

I dreamt, that night, of ghosts asking us to please stop trying to appropriate their ghost culture.

6.

We drove past a sign in Chinatown that said:
Chair
Table
Booth

I said I repeat it to myself like a mantra—and felt relieved when you did not laugh.

7.

We looked at a picture of orphaned bats in swaddling clothes. We said we'd be their parents if we could. I pictured their baby-bat voices, triangulating, ricocheting off of walls. I read that bats, dying, dry up like crumbling flowers and leaves.

8.

There was another supermoon. There was another full moon. There was a pink moon, and I tried out ghost language myself: *Do you really think that this is the only place left to live?*

9.

Everyone crawled around, hunched in, protecting soft, vulnerable internal organs. We were all unaware of our own potentials. A doldrums mentality seemed the only way to think. I dreamt of ghosts saying, *If you are going to live, you cannot stay here!*

10.

I drew a picture of a shiso leaf. I cut tiny holes in the paper. I held it up to the window so light shone through in pale pinks, greens, yellows, blues. It was 1:11, 3:33, 5:55.

I said aloud: I am sending energy to you that I am—that I am—but could not finish the sentence.

11.

I dreamt of ghosts as vessels, whispering words they did not comprehend:
You do have energy!
There is no depletion!
There is no disorder!
It's not too late!
There is no "it."

12.

I dreamt of a hazy girl in a drafty house, standing amidst dust motes in the molecular air. She inscribed lists of numbers on a pad of paper. Faded pencil; neat, even rows.

She was a version of the woman I'd loved. The one who toppled off the edge of the earth.

13.

I thought that *somehow* is one of the saddest words in the human language—and also the kindest.

I decided that, really, I did not have to put away my own damage.

I understood that I did not get to decide how or even *whether*.

14.

I realized that sequences of numbers are unchained energy. Flying minds trying to refocus, recombine. It is here that the dead can visit the living. And for a brief time, pin themselves back to the earth.

15.

I remembered that the best possible outcome includes everything.

I decided that I shouldn't unwrite anything as it is happening.

I understood that there was never going to be a different story— or maybe there was, but this is the one that happened.

16.

A hard-sharp noise, the hit-head dullness of the high-summer middle of a day. Head-swimming in the sun filtering through gauzy curtains, our bodies pressed together, sweating freely, forgetting to hold my stomach in, in the afternoon.

I whispered, without meaning to: *I, just, please.* I looked at you quickly, but you were asleep.

I heard a woman outside, asking: *How can hail form in this heat?*

—and then answering herself: *It comes from a place where it is cold enough to form, then drops through the clouds.*

Far away, a man shouted, *It's not crystallized yet!*

A mixture of late-day light and bird shadows, and maybe everything real seems grossly symbolic in the telling—weighted and heavy in meaning. I might have to spend the rest of my life trying to unwrite and unravel, until all of the threads float free in the breeze.

17.

I thought about how sometimes I feel like most of my soul has been plucked away, leaving a tattered scrap, a dirty, once-red rag blowing in the wind—then remembered that just the day before, I'd figured out that wasn't true.

Outside the window, a little girl whispered, urgently, *Please, ease.*

After a little while, she sang: *Swinging, swinging, over the Milky Way!*

—and then corrected herself:
swimming, swimming,
  la la la la la la!

18.

A calm, warm day, summer in my childhood. I looked out the kitchen window at faraway hills, blue-gray. I imagined I was a giant creature—gangly daddy-long-legs appendages, leaping from hill to hill. I was eating bread at the wooden table, seeds on my tongue, but somewhere else, also, flying.

19.

A girl lay on the table in a doctor's office, her arms at her sides. *A bier*, she thought. *A coffin.* But at the same time, she felt safe, ensconced. The silk-lined case in a doll museum. Either way, every time, it always came back to this: her lying on her back. The domed pink ceiling.

Today, she thought of pebbles, heavy and smooth, resting on her arms and legs, her stomach. She heard a voice, its lilting sing-song—*the stones and the shore*—some indistinct humming. A second refrain about bodyless fingers. These lyrics made it clear that the stuffing had been removed from the fingers' interiors. It was only straw. Just hay.

The ceiling was gone. In its place, twigs and branches.

20.

I lay in a narrow bed, in a narrow room, feeling myself borne forth. The sun shone in, gentle and warm. Nothing horrible, nothing tragic.

I thought about how something keeps taking people and slamming them against the fabric of the earth—.

And also that it is trying to shake from them something good. Something already there to begin with.

21.

I walked through a deli, my dog on a leash, looking for something to drink. We turned a corner, and, suddenly: a cat with a mouse in its mouth. The cat let its mouth drop open, and out fell the mouse—dead, or maybe just stunned.

For one brief moment, everything froze: cat, mouth open; mouse on the floor; my dog, pushed against my leg; and me—all a queasy tilt-sway under the fluorescent lights.

There was a pause, and then a beat.

I knew, then, that everything was going to be fine. Something sent. Something I could use one day, but not quite yet.

22.

Rear headlights glowed like owls' eyes as we drove over a bridge. The sun was setting, burning pinks, oranges, yellows into the water of the river. It filtered through the car window, stitching over your face.

I thought about how I would never forget how you looked in that moment—your hand warm in my lap, your face to the side, sleeping, as my eyes squinted and closed in the embroidered light.

23.

Something you said, then, when you woke up: *Aren't you glad to be human?*

Nancy Chen Long

Why I Should Love the Number 8

Oxygen has eight protons, eight
neutrons, eight electrons. Without
oxygen, the newborn couldn't
struggle to take her first breath, arch
then wail when air finally hits
her lungs. Three eights—trinity
of infinities turned sideways,
a tripled prosperity. Eight—

number steeped in good luck, held high
by the Chinese, and genetic
predispositions, some say, are
immutable, my behavior
foretold like sunrise. Should I dream
of *8* as I do the dying and
fevered Betelgeuse, eighth brightest
star in the dark heavens? *Eight maids*

a-milking for *Eight Days a Week.*
An elegant biology:
Picture *spiders*. *Octopi*. See
the eight-spotted forester, four
white spheres on each blackened wing. Think
teeth, eight housed in each quadrant of
our mouths, the eighth one named *wisdom*
tooth, something we tend to cut out.

Anthony Borruso

Sad Little Anthony

look at you, hardly an outline
in this dark room, this dark time
of recovery. poor little anthony,

they cut you up good:
a bit of skull, a slice of spine.
you've draped beach towels

over the blinds, you sink
into a black lake. let sleep
smooth you like a zamboni

over scarred ice. let darkness
scrub the blood from your head.
when dad's spoon goes clink,

clink in a bowl and the whole
world quivers with clinks, crawl
into yourself, shivering, skinny,

hungry, here, let's fill you
with oxtail soup and oxycodone,
poetry and sympathy. poor

anthony, clench your teeth.
no one feels so bad for you
as you, and that makes us sad.

Anthony Borruso

Staten Island

Island of buzz cuts, fades, and tape-ups,
nail parlors, tanning salons, pizzerias
that sell by the slice. Island of callery pears

that bloom and stink of bad sex, Honda Civics,
paint-chipped handball courts, Arizona tallboys.
Island of roaches and joints, ice cream trucks singing,

slinging oxycodone. Island of stained glass
churches, false awakenings: dullards staking
claims on a post-life, Jesus at a juice bar,

flaking flaxseed in his smoothie, downing shots
of wheatgrass. Hipster island, Guido island,
black island, white island, island of my dad's a cop,

it won't happen again, officer. I-take-two-trains-
and-a-ferry-to-work island. Island of suburban bliss,
as south as you can get in this city, driver's license

suspended, mother-in-law rear-ended,
football captains flunking trade school.
Island of callused hands and radioactive parks,

panicked teachers praying for a pay raise,
slate-faced junkies, pin-striped suits at yacht clubs
clinking drinks with amnesiac immigrants. Glass-lipped

island, blue-ache island, island of don't park
in front of my house, peach-glow alcove island,
late-night bocci ball island, rickety boardwalks

and salty breezes, crushed Four Lokos.
Island of the osprey perched on the highest branch at Gateway beach.
Island of nervous breakdowns, a city that thinks

it's a small town, the forgotten borough,
Staten Italy, island of the white-tailed doe
and the candelabra-capped buck. Island of I'll never

come back, island of I always come back.
Island of second chances. Island of my love,
her woeful hips, our lip-locked afterglow.

Joseph Harris

You're in the Wrong Place

When Glen didn't show up for work we assumed he was out all night again, that he'd meet up after breakfast wearing his wraparound sunglasses, reeking of Skin Bracer to hide the smell. I'd thought about heading over to his house to rouse him, but I hadn't been there in years, and, besides, I could barely see through *my* hangover. So Billy, Ray, and I poured Kessler into our coffee and toasted, "To Glen— fuck'm."

Before this landscaping season, we'd been short on work since Dynamic Fabricating, that old shop on Hilton Road just north of the Detroit city limits, went under and took most of our clients with it—former Dynamic employees all.

Then, in March, the bank that owned the property called. Wanted us to "maintain the grounds" of Dynamic until they could find a buyer. The first day on the job, Glen motioned me over to the front door with a languid swing of his arm. Someone had spray-painted: IF YOU'RE LOOKING FOR WORK, YOU'RE IN THE WRONG PLACE.

We thought that was funny as hell. Particularly the correct punctuation—probably some smartass who dropped out of college to get a paycheck, someone who thought all that "opportunity" talk about acquiring a humanities degree in a post-industrial economy was bullshit … someone like me, I guess, even though I would never have had the balls to tag the façade of some rotting factory. Anyway, we took to saying it all the time. It helped break the day up.

And in May, the bank called again: another contract to maintain the lawns of the foreclosed houses in the neighborhood—the houses of all our former clients. Standard cut, edging, too, weeding if there were gardens.

After downing the coffee, the three of us stopped at a gas station to fill up the equipment and grab a few snacks. It took half the time without Glen harassing the attendant with his fucking lottery numbers. Billy walked out with a scratch-off, asked me to do the honors with his lucky nickel. I rubbed off the film and gasped.

"No way!" Ray said, chewing on an apple in his sun-faded U of M English T-shirt.

"How much, Dick?" said Billy, lifting up his dirty Tigers hat and running his hands through his greasy hair.

"Billy," I smiled and tossed him the loser, "if you're looking for winners, you're in the wrong place."

The first group of homes we hit was behind Dynamic and the train tracks that emptied out into the sprawling Canadian National train yard. These were the rentals and starter homes, 500-700 square feet, two-bedroom bungalows with no garages. Even without Glen, we could do a whole place—front, back, edging—in under five minutes. We zig-zagged through the neighborhood from north to south, stopping to sip coffee and eat Swiss Rolls behind the shuttered warehouses that faced 8 Mile.

"You worried about Glen?" Billy asked me, stirring in a ripped packet of Splenda.

"Can't tell if he's been hitting it more than usual," I said, though with Glen (and me, and Billy, I guess), it was always hard to tell. Landscaping attracts a certain kind of temperament. High turnover, mostly drifters with substance-abuse problems (like Glen) or college kids working summers to save up for tuition hikes (like Ray) or burned-out retail workers who can't stand another holiday season stocking perfume or selling vacuums, making half of what they did at Dynamic (like Billy). After Easter you worked until the first post-Thanksgiving freeze then started back up when the last March thaw turned everything to mud.

I loved the life—loved watching the seasons change, loved the camaraderie, loved that I could drink and gamble every day and no one said shit. That's why I dropped out of college—I couldn't stand the smugness, the elitism. I didn't want a fucking "life of the mind"—I wanted to work outside. Glen was a drinking buddy of my dad's, said he'd give me a shot in his operation. I took it, and for three years we fell into the rhythm: up at 6 a.m., breaks at 9, 12, and 3, punching out at 6 p.m. and staying at the bar till the Tigers game was over or Glen blew the last of the day's earnings on Jameson shots and side bets on pool games.

"That's just who he is," I said to Billy, who drained his coffee in one fluid gulp. "He's never been a morning person."

The clock hit 9 a.m., and the night shift at the only open warehouse walked out into the murky sunshine. Billy recognized one of them. "Johnny Boy!"

Johnny Boy shielded his eyes and walked over to us, his filthy sweatshirt billowing from the gusts of passing semis.

"This motherfucker used to work at Dynamic with me," Billy said, chewing the filter of a Pall Mall. Ray, as usual, buried his head in a yellowed paperback copy of *Capital*.

"So, how's this gig?" I asked.

"They got us on twelve-hour days, man. Fuckin' eight bucks an hour. Thirty minutes for lunch. It's borderline criminal, I'm telling you."

Billy swallowed a laugh. "Johnny, if you're looking for sympathy …."

I didn't know the prick, so I passed on the punch line, but Ray, ever eager to earn his working-class bona fides, chimed in, right on cue: "You're in the wrong place."

We raced up Wanda to 9 Mile then took a left till we reached Campbell Heights. The neighborhood was filled with overgrown gardens, grown mostly by Dynamic retirees who had seen their pensions sucked up when the owners filed for bankruptcy protection. So we pulled out the pruners and the mulch and got our hands dirty.

We were clearing a shade garden when Ray noticed a bald man in a black smock walking an old lady up her front porch across the street.

"Hey, it's a fucking priest," Billy said.

Indeed, it was. Ray wiped sod from his eyes. "Which one is he again? Father …."

"Fuck if I know," Billy said. "I stopped going after I got confirmed. That purgatory bullshit really rubbed me the wrong way. What a bunch of fucking nonsense. Besides, there's no way I'm nursing my hangover during mass, you know what I mean?"

Ray called out to him. "Hey, Father!"

He turned to us. "Good morning, boys." He blessed us.

"Be nice, Billy," I said.

The priest adjusted his glasses, looked at me. "Richard? Richard Piscek?"

"That's right. How are you, Father?"

"I haven't seen you since your confirmation."

Billy laughed. "I bet this guy fuckin' baptized you, too," he whispered to me.

"He did," I said.

"Well, we'd love to see you at mass again. People really need it, since that factory closed."

"I'll go with you," Ray said, full of that Protestant fascination with my lapsed pagan faith. It pissed me right off, almost as much as having to take Glen to see his bookie on football Sundays if he was too drunk to drive. And where was he, anyway?

"All are welcome in the house of God," the priest said.

Billy couldn't help himself. "Hey, Father!"

"Yes, son?"

"If you're looking for converts, you're in the wrong place."

East of the factory were the bigger houses with bigger lawns— additions tucked in to the front of the lots all the way up the sidewalk, fire pits growing moss in the back, surrounded by rusted folding chairs. Edging out front took some time—so did pruning the fucking fire pits, throwing the rotten wood through our mobile chipper. I kept having to remove jams from Ray throwing them in too quickly and found dozens of scratch-offs. Probably Glen's or Billy's—that's the first thing they did with their paychecks every Friday.

When we reached the corner of Paxton and Cambourne, we saw three young guys dressed in black and red: a fat one with a drum, a lanky one with a sign, a balding one with a loudspeaker. They were down from Ann Arbor on assignment from one of their Marxist professors, extra credit or some bullshit like that. Friends of Ray, apparently—they shook hands.

"We're protesting the unlawful seizure of this property and others like it," said the one with the sign.

"You don't say." Billy grinned, lit a cigarette.

"The capitalist superstructure is collapsing," said the one with the loudspeaker, "and with your help, we can usher in better world for the working man." The one with the drum executed a low rattle of support.

I appreciated the sentiment, but I didn't need some smarmy U of M dickhead to tell me how fucked I was. These kids had never "worked" in the "proletarian" sense, and they'd never have to. It reminded me of myself a few years ago—a kid with a college savings account paid for by some grandparent's factory work, the opportunity to join the New Economy I threw away.

"Hey, kid," said Billy. "If you're looking for solidarity …."

I finished that one off; there's nothing I hate more than bourgeois offspring pretending to be Walter Reuther. "You're in the wrong place."

In the truck between houses, Ray went on and on about this event he was organizing for the fall semester back in Ann Arbor: some kind of town-hall discussion about the loss of faith and work in post-industrial society, how we lived in an indifferent universe and that it all presented some kind of philosophical problem.

"So let me get this straight," Billy said, draining a Gatorade. "You're saying that we gave up God when we got money, and that now that we don't got no money, we can't go back to believing because … why, again?"

Ray sat up, finished his last stick of jerky. Across the street, we made out a cadre of young DUIs riding their childhood bikes to the liquor store, still wearing their blue Dynamic work shirts. "Well, we've disproved the existence of another world, haven't we? But we can't disprove the existence of capital—it touches every single aspect of our lives, not just in terms of the financial but the familial, even sexual. In unionized industrial societies, we could manufacture meaning through labor, creating wealth and purchasing the physical and emotional materials to build meaning without religion: a better life. But now, with religion gone and labor gone, what's left?"

When Dynamic went under, Glen and I were out at the bar after he'd lost five hundred dollars in a poker game to some local scumbag—Jerry was his name, I think—and Glen was telling me the difference between wants and needs. "Everyone who worked at that place, all they had was wants," he said, "all they had were dreams of what to do with that money. And now it's all fucking gone—now it's all gonna be needs, from here on out."

And as Ray went on about all his theoretical bullshit, I wondered if any of it would help Glen—help Billy, help me.

Billy didn't even wait till he was finished. "Ray, my man, if you're looking for transcendence ...."

I decided to chime in again. The whiskey was wearing off and I remembered how stupid I thought Ray was, slumming it up with us during his break from school, even though his family was poorer than mine. My dad never had to work at Dynamic—his did. "You're in the wrong place."

We went to the bar for lunch, chased our cheeseburger with beer and took a shot for Glen. On the TV, some star-crossed lovers my age—arrogant young doctors or lawyers or something ridiculous like that—pleaded with one another that they needed time to sort things out, to figure out who they *really were.*

"Easy on the lotto tickets," I called to Billy. "Clogged the fucking chipper."

"The fuck are you talking about? I keep all mine. Sooner or later, you find your pattern."

"That wasn't you?"

"Dick, my friend, if you're looking for advice ...."

"Can we drop it for lunch, fellas?" Ray was sorting his money—his girlfriend was driving over from Grand Rapids, and they were heading across the river to Windsor for the night to go drinking and gambling, just like I did when I was nineteen. "It's kinda getting on my nerves."

"What would you know about nerves, college boy?" I sneered. The rich, young lovers talked about their plethora of coastal opportunities, gesticulating theatrically that they *didn't want to live with regrets.*

"Must be nice," mumbled some bearded drunk next to me.

"Fuckin' right," I said.

"Can you imagine if someone started talking like that around here?"

I drained my beer. "If you're looking for self-actualization ...."

"You heard the kid," Billy laughed from the Keno machine.

I tapped the drunk on the shoulder to buy him a shot, then caught a look at his face.

"Bobby? Bobby Kowolski?"

"In the fucking flesh." He put his head back down and snored. The bartender poured us shots and motioned with his head to a sign that said, "The one and only rule: no sleeping at the bar."

"How the fuck are you?" I hadn't seen him since we graduated high school—must have been five, six years.

"I'm still here."

I put the shot in front of him. "Cheers, you son of a bitch."

He took the shot and perked up.

"I thought you were at Western?" Bobby was the star point guard on our basketball team, got a full ride to college.

He pulled up his dirty sweatpants and showed me the map of scars on his knee. "Not anymore. Kept tearing cartilage. Flunked out after the injuries and got a job at Dynamic. Now I'm here."

The characters on the TV started crying. Billy walked over and put a hand on my shoulder. "So this is what Ray has to look forward to, huh?"

"Fuck Ray," I said as Ray walked out.

Billy laughed. "Well, if you're looking for love ...."

So it was just Billy and me hitting the afternoon houses, to the south of Dynamic—the desperate ones, rotted and overgrown, the ones that were about to be condemned by the city.

The first one—a new house on the list, added by the bank that very day—was really something: grass not cut for at least a year, rising up past my thighs; ivy crawling over the smudged windows; dandelions and clover poking through the walkway gaps. It looked familiar, maybe one I cut a few years ago, but with my buzz on I couldn't remember.

I yanked the cord of my weed whacker, and someone burst through the front door with an aluminum baseball bat.

It was Glen—sweat-stained shirt untucked, popped buttons exposing his distended stomach.

"Get *outta* here, you motherfuckers!" He went after the power mower first, Billy splitting as soon as Glen charged. He dented the hood then lifted the gas tank, smashed the engine. I dropped my weed whacker and pleaded with him.

"Glen! Glen! It's fucking us, man! It's me!"

"You think you can just take my fucking property! Fuck you! I'll fucking wreck it all before you take it!" I tried to catch his eyes, but they were bloodshot without his glasses.

As he smashed the mower to pieces, I looked inside the house and saw hundreds of empty beer cans, some stuffed with scratch-offs, some with slips from the Hazel Park racetrack, some with parking tickets from the casinos downtown: Greektown, Motor City, MGM. "Why didn't you tell me? I could have …."

"Could have done what?" He leered at me, cheeks slick with tears. "You ever have a fucking problem, kid? A *real* fucking problem?"

"Glen, put the bat down …."

"And how do you know my name? Who sent you here? You with Jerry? The credit card company? The fucking bank? Get the fuck off my property!"

"Glen, it's not yours anymore." I heard sirens down the street. Someone with a decent mortgage must have called the police.

"The fuck it isn't!" Then the cops pulled up behind him and wrestled him to the ground, cuffed him. The whole time he kept screaming, "You don't need it, you bastard, you son of a bitch, you don't need it!" and I could have sworn he was staring right at me.

With our stuff smashed up, we went back to the bar. None of it was insured, so I thought I'd get drunk and not think about what we were gonna tell Ray tomorrow or how I was gonna pay *my* mortgage. On the TV, the Tigers were warming up for a West Coast day game. I felt around for the sweaty ball of money in my jeans and thought about needs. Bobby was still glued to his barstool, trying to stay awake. Billy tried to cajole me into a dart game, but I waved him off. I was too bothered by that thing with Glen to aim right.

I ordered another shot. Billy yelled something from the jukebox, but I couldn't hear.

I mean, where the fuck did Glen get off? Calling me spoiled. Sure, maybe I was, but not now—not thanks to him. Some cheerful Motown song drained out through the jukebox speakers, and Billy yelled, "Hey, Dick! You deaf? I said, 'If you're looking for work ….'"

The Missouri State University Student Literary Competitions

Moon City Review is a journal published by the Department of English at Missouri State University. *MCR* publishes one poem and one fiction work annually by its student population, as selected in a competition inititially by our own faculty, and then finally by an outside judge. For the first time this year, we have added a creative nonfiction competition as well.

For our initial creative nonfiction contest, Donald Quist—author of the essay collection *Harbors*—selected Amanda Hadlock's essay, "Death Only Happens Once in a Lifetime." Of Hadlock's essay, Quists remarks,

> I greatly admire this prose, the ways in which the narrative examines conflicts of class and culture while never becoming didactic or prescriptive. The writing is deft, nuanced, and graceful in the depiction of its subjects. This essay achieves a sense of commonality in its specific descriptions of working-class poverty in relation to family, music, and ideology. I was immediately captured by the voice: clear, thoughtful, distant but not detached. It's an essay packed with poignant scenes.

Other finalists considered in the creative nonfiction category include the following writers: Sarah Bachler, Sarah Harp, Brian Illum, Ryan LaBee, Alexis McCoy, and Kyle Osredker.

In fiction, Kim Magowan—author of *Undoing: Stories,* winner of the 2017 Moon City Short Fiction Award—chose Taylor Jim Sly's story "Pants on Fire" for the first prize. Magowan says,

> In "Pants on Fire," a crew of friends tell tall tales about someone who tells tall tales: They revile absent Brandon Sandridge because, as the narrator puts it, "He gets such a pass for being a liar." But the story also asks, probingly and acutely, why those lies unsettle them so: "'What personal achievements of yours have been jeopardized by Brandon's stories?'" one character demands. This is a funny, poignant, strangely tender story

about why people need to skewer storytellers and what lies of omission those truth-enforcers tell themselves.

Joining Sly as finalists were Lucien Curtis, Amelia Fisher, Madison Green, Katelyn Grisham, Josh Henderson, Kristan Key, John King, Kathleen Powell, and Shannon Wick.

Finally, in poetry, guest judge Erin Hoover—author of *Barnburner,* winner of the Elixir Press' Antivenom Award—chose David Herghelegiu's "The First Baptist, the Last Amen" as the winner. Of Herghelegiu's poem, Hoover notes,

> "The First Baptist, the Last Amen" distills two lives into a scant nineteen lines. Yet the poem's brevity is also one of its strengths, as each line offers the reward of new disclosure. The punishment borne by a religious ancestor resonates against the modern-day "stoning" of the self, a suicide attempt that serves as the locus of the poem, caused by the speaker's internalization of faith-based intolerance. I am grateful for the way this poem asked me to think deeply about the affirmation contained in the simple word *Amen* about the relationship between what we affirm and what we reject, and about surviving within and despite a caustic belief system.

MCR also would like to congratulate the other finalists considered in the poetry category; they include Lisa Anthony, Daren Colbert, Charlie Crane, Jenny Crews, Madison Green, and Brooke Matejka.

It was a great pleasure for everyone involved to sort out the students' work. We are proud to present the winning selections in the following pages.

Amanda Hadlock

Death Only Happens Once in a Lifetime

December 20, 2016.

You were working at a lingerie boutique in a dingy southwest Missouri mall when your step-grandmother called to mention the hospice nurse pronounced Grandpa dead that morning. His lung cancer had finally stiffed him. You weren't surprised; you'd been bracing for it since the bleak diagnosis in June. But knowing doesn't ease the blow when it hits.

You'd been at work for going on nine hours. You'd been helping an elderly woman with chronic arthritis in her fingers put on a bra. She complimented your patience and called you sweet. She stroked your smooth twenty-year-old hand with her horribly disfigured ones as you handed her the receipt.

You made 6 percent commission on her $114 purchase after upselling the exclusive delicate laundry soap. Paraben and dye free, with the refreshing scent of lavender. You added on a pair of control-top panties, too, at the modest price of $27 a pop. She only bought one bra, a binding, Band-Aid colored elastic thing that awkwardly hugged her sloped shoulders and sunken chest. It didn't look comfortable, but it was the only one she could manage to wrestle on without help. She said she had no one at home who would be able to help her hook a different one. "Don't get old," she said. "Stay young forever. These are the happiest days of your life." You offered a kind of half-laugh; these "happiest days" felt more exhausting than anything.

She said "God bless you" as she walked away. She waved good-bye with warped fingers, her knuckles knotted like tree roots, warped wood, her hands painfully gnarled and tangled. You smiled and waved back, a flippant toss of your arm in the air. In retrospect, your fingers wiggling freely like that must have seemed taunting to her. Condescending. Inconsiderate. You never saw her again.

Then Grandma called the store phone and said Grandpa's dead, and could you let your brother and mother know, please?

Oh. OK. Yes.

Click.

December 23, 2016.

It was raining on your way to Grandpa's funeral. The cliché made you laugh to yourself. Your mother sparked a cigarette in the car (Kools Menthol, if it matters). You hadn't seen her for six years until the diagnosis. No one had. Then suddenly, one day in late October, she showed up on a Greyhound bus and started staying on your brother's couch. Talk about a role reversal. She'd been God-knows-where, living her life riding around on bicycles with her boyfriend in Kansas City, she claims. Most likely still on a mix of meth and opiates, like she was the last time you saw her, when you were fourteen and watched her being hauled away in handcuffs. You came home from school that day to find her and the aforementioned boyfriend high, screaming, and throwing furniture at each other (again). So you called 911 from the neighbor's landline. You were finally fed up. The neighbor offered a half-hearted "sorry" for the fact he was going to let it slide, though inevitably he had overheard for quite some time. Your mom and the boyfriend were arrested (again). You and your brother then moved in with a friend's parents to finish out high school in the suburban Kansas City town you lived in before you both moved to Springfield for college. But now you were stuck hauling dear old Mom to her father's funeral. She couldn't legally drive there, and that's a damn long way to bike. You figured death only happens once in a lifetime and you shouldn't keep her away from her own father's funeral, no matter how absent she'd chosen to be from your lives. No matter how negligent she was of her father's illness until she heard there might be some inheritance money involved once his farmhouse was sold if she showed up and offered him a good-bye before he croaked.

The truck in front of you on the highway boasted a bright orange bumper sticker: "HEY OBAMA: REDISTRIBUTE THIS" and a hand flipping the bird to everyone in the world. You hate this part of the country sometimes. The buckle of the Bible Belt. You see red everywhere you look. This was a little less than a month before Trump's inauguration, and the climate was especially bad. Of course, having grown up poor, you are especially attuned to the extreme socioeconomic stratification in America. Your suburban hometown was especially bad, with the drugs and poverty masked by dominant middle-class standards. You wish you could've pulled the bumper sticker guy over, told him you're one of 44 million Americans who don't have health insurance, you haven't been to a dentist since you were sixteen since you can't afford it, your wisdom teeth sit in the back of your jaws constantly scraping your gums, too expensive to remove, you work two jobs fifty hours a week to meet basic survival needs on top of full-time college that's barely covered by a Pell Grant and loans. You want to tell him you work for everything you have, you feel entitled to nothing. You want to tell him about the times as a kid when your mom would neglect the utility bills (again) and you'd be left filling the big soup pot with water from the neighbor's hose and boiling it to take a bath.

You have a slew of Crazy Mom Stories™, you casually tell people at parties sometimes. Like the time you were thirteen and Mom was going through opiate withdrawals and ran outside stark naked at 2 a.m. to throw rocks at the neighbor's window. The neighbor called the cops (duh), and you remember a police officer taking you and your brother to see her while she detoxed in the hospital; her wrists and ankles were shackled to the bed, her limbs limply spread like she was a frog pinned down for dissection. She always did lash out a lot. Like the time you walked home from play practice in ninth grade, since she'd forgotten to pick you up, and when you opened the door a hot skillet full of Hamburger Helper whizzed by your face (she was throwing it at the boyfriend). Or the times she'd leave for weeks, a feeble ration of Vienna sausage and fruit cocktail stacked on the counter for her kids. Or the times she'd steal your brother's car (which he bought with money he'd earned working at McDonald's since his fifteenth birthday) until the time she totaled it. Or the times she'd beg her dad for money, "For the kiddos," and turn around and give it all to her dealer. Or the times she'd show up tweaking and twist your hair in her fist and drag you around after your accusations of her addiction, which she claimed everyone was imagining. Or the times ....

The truck disappeared as you exited the highway. You took a deep breath and rolled down your window to clear the smoke. You finally arrived at the funeral home.

"Here goes nothing," you said as you parked, finally breaking the silence.

Everyone cried at the funeral like they were supposed to. It was well attended. Your grandfather was a respected cattle farmer out in Bolivar. You passed the time counting all the cowboy boots that passed you by. Turquoise and snakeskin and scuffed brown leather. You lost track at forty-one. (Can that be right?) There was a framed picture on the casket of Grandpa shaking hands with Harry Truman. You smirked at it, knowing how big of a "pansy" Grandpa thought Truman was. The president had recognized Grandpa's advocacy work for Missouri farmers' rights. "I may be the poorest man whose boot heels ever hit the White House floor," Grandpa said with a mostly toothless grin when he'd told you the story years ago. Or something like that. Your aunt and uncle mostly ignored their sister, your mother. Your step-grandmother cried into a Kleenex next to you, hugging everyone who passed. Your brother held Grandma's hand the whole time. You sat with your arms crossed and eyes closed in an attempt to hide your tears. Your mother hammed it up, sobbed loudly, snot oozing, and tried to appear normal, as if she'd had any semblance of a relationship with her father the last six years of his life. A farmer friend of your grandfather's approached her at one point, offered his condolences. "You're his youngest?" the man asked. "Yes," she said, tears still dripping. He narrowed his eyes, had a knowing look, just walked away after that.

You could feel the room's eyes on you. "Everyone knows me as the Crazy One's kid," you thought. (Again.)

At the end, a song played. "There's Nothing I Can Do About It Now" by Willie Nelson. Grandpa had requested it. He had a dark sense of humor. The last lines stay with you: *I'm forgiving everything that forgiveness will allow / And there's nothing I can do about it now ....*

December 24, 2016.

You and your brother spent Christmas Eve at your step-grandmother's house. Your mother wasn't invited. You have no clue what she did that day, probably don't want to imagine it.

Your step-grandmother's family is huge; you vaguely remembered having met some of them at some point before in your childhood, a distant, hazy Thanksgiving memory, or perhaps a birthday or Christmas Eve past. But their faces blend together; they all look the same. All attractive brunettes with a gaggle of kids, her daughters with well-to-do husbands, her sons with beauty-queen wives. Children chased each other in new shoes and clothes, their parents gently scolding them not to ruin their holiday outfits. Everything your family never was and never will be.

You and your brother watched for a while, not making much conversation, before you made your way to Grandpa's old room. You perused his bookshelf, mostly old Western paperbacks. You flipped through some photo albums, lots of black-and-white snapshots of him in his old Air Force fatigues. Lots of pictures of your uncle, your aunt, and your mom when they were kids. They all had crooked 70s bowl cuts and overalls. In one photo, your grandfather smiled next to his first wife—your mom's mom, your grandma—on a paisley couch. Grandma Juanita passed away before you were born, the story goes. She had debilitating Type 2 Diabetes and died in a diabetic coma. Maybe that's where so much of your mother's pain stems from, you think. As you flipped through your grandfather's memories, you and your brother tried not to think of your mother, of how you'd have to deal with her through all the legal bullshit that follows someone's death. How she'd probably take her dead dad's money and run, go back to the boyfriend and squander it all on drugs. (Sure enough, she would.) You tried not to think of how some people are simply beyond saving despite everyone's best efforts, how people have to save themselves. You tried not to think of it. You tried.

You came across Grandpa's record collection. You found a title you recognized, pulled it out and blew the dust off. *A Horse Called Music*, by Willie Nelson. You put it on, dropped the needle to the vinyl. A song started, slow and scratchy at first, but beautiful, nostalgic. Those last lines still stick in your head: *I'm forgiving everything that forgiveness will allow / And there's nothing I can do about it now ....*

Taylor Jim Sly

Pants on Fire

OK, let's start from the beginning.

Tanner Hedgepeth said that when Brandon Sandridge was born, he didn't cry. His eyes were wide open and the first thing he did was turn his head in the embrace of the attending and wink at a nurse.

I heard Brandon Sandridge learned to speak by eaves-watching *60 Minutes* from his crib. Apparently his first words were "ammunition" and "collateralized debt obligation."

Word is Brandon Sandridge taught himself to play jazz drums by listening to passing traffic and replicating it on pots and pans. He said his babysitter still has a video of it.

One time I heard that Brandon Sandridge went on his first family vacation to the Grand Canyon and managed to tame and ride two coyotes. He coaxed them into submission with outstretched palms and a bologna sandwich.

I heard Brandon Sandridge is actually four years younger than us. His parents took him to preschool when he was still in diapers because they felt like they'd already run out of things to teach him and they let him skip, like, a few grades.

Remember when all those fire trucks showed up at the back of the school during recess in second grade? I heard Brandon Sandridge was doing a science experiment with a magnifying glass and some weapons-grade plutonium his dad had laying around and he set fire to the Dumpster receptacle.

My sister said she kissed Brandon Sandridge behind the school bus when we were still in grade school and she said his lips were so soft you could sink into them. Like *clouds*—her words!

Brandon Sandridge knows how to count cards and can beat you in any game, blackjack, aces high, go fish, you name it. Word is he was being scouted by the Professional Poker League.

Brandon Sandridge fell into the lake one summer and got attacked by a crappie the size of a used Buick. He had his pocketknife on him, though, and some of the pieces he filleted got tangled up in the kelp on the shoreline? He tried one and was, like, "Hey, that's good, I like that." And just like that, *snap* Brandon Sandridge invented sushi.

Bra—. Oh, thank you … Brandon Sandridge … the word is that guy trained with SEAL Team Six. They came and took him from his mom one summer and he went to the Ural Mountains in *Siberia*. I've heard he has scars on his upper thigh, above the pant line, from where he got bit by one of those huge dire wolves.

I heard the Daytona 500 was won a while back by a mysterious driver who wore his helmet the whole time so you couldn't see his face. Brandon's never come out and said it was him, but then no one's been able to put the two in the same room at the same time.

Brandon Sandridge spent the entire summer before middle school learning to program and hack. I've been told that if you want *infinite* X-Box Live credits, go to him. Apparently he has a guy on the inside at Microsoft who jailbroke his console and gave him something he called "X-Box Live *Black*."

Brandon Sandridge has the biggest dick known to man.

I heard in middle school that Brandon Sandridge got invited backstage at Warped Tour to hang out with Miss May I. I think his brother knew the bass player and they hit it off really well. Brandon knew all of their first names. He said they smoked weed before their set.

Apparently Brandon has an uncle up in Maine that owns an *actual castle*. Brandon's spent some time up there. I've heard it's pretty sweet, but he complains about the drafts.

You know how freshman year Brandon Sandridge drove that piece-of-shit Civic? Word is that's just his *day* car; he keeps a brand new 2012 McLaren F1 in a special atmosphere-sealed garage for when he wants to go out on the town.

I heard Katy Stevens broke up with Brandon when she found out he'd been texting a supermodel from England. Brandon said it was easy to get nudes 'cause she had those fucked-up British teeth and low self-esteem but a *really* bangin' bod.

Brandon Sandridge has, for a fact, flown an F-18 Super Hornet. His granddad was in the Air Force during Vietnam and he knew some people who let him go on base and test drive one out over the Pacific

Northwest. I guess he did so well that the guys in charge invited him to join up there and then but Brandon declined 'cause he had school on Monday.

Brandon Sandridge was, for a time, the youngest member of Anonymous.

Remember that big apartment fire junior year that killed, like, three people? Brandon Sandridge wasn't there, but that same night I guess he was the first responder to a car that drove off into a ravine and stopped the guy's neck from bleeding until the paramedics got there.

Brandon's dad went to high school with Brad Pitt and one day at the range Brandon taught him how to shoot a gun. You'd think from all the acting and the Midwestern background he'd have picked that up somewhere, but you'd be dead wrong.

Fuuuuck yeah, who put this song on?

Brandon Sandridge had to stop competing in the MMA because he stopped the heart of a guy in his weight class with one punch.

I heard Brandon Sandridge reads Wittgenstein on the john. For *fun*.

Word is that Brandon Sandridge installed nitrous in his car and has been the employee of the month for Postmates two years running.

There's a video floating around out there of Brandon Sandridge doing a quintuple backflip on a trampoline on a day that he didn't take his meds.

Brandon Sandridge is the only person I know who got a standing ovation on his SAT.

Brandon Sandridge has a secret rap career under a moniker he won't tell us, but he's been featured on Eminem songs.

Brandon Sandridge has, can, and will steal your girl.

"OK, you guys are a bunch of *assholes*."

Our drunken circle tessellates into turns, leans, and scooches in order to see our dissident. Hey, it's Karen O'Dell and she's standing in the kitchen doorway with an expression of secondhand offense while a house party thunders behind her.

"What? It's all part of the canon." Mark squints his eyes and points an index finger pulled from his Rolling Rock. "Or are you saying that Brandon Sandridge might be ... lying to us?"

We shock ourselves with how quickly and successful we pantomime being aghast.

Karen's head tips to two o'clock as she scoffs. "You are such a dick, Mark. You know what he's like."

"Yeah," I pipe up from near the back, "From what I've heard he's a fucking rockstar."

"Fuck you, Devin. I can't believe you're making fun of him."

"*What?* No we're not, we're reminiscing. If anything we're, like, *minstrels*, recounting his deeds of bravery. Right, boys?

The minstrels agree.

"The guy *clearly* has issues. He can't help it." Karen looks like she did when she was six, only longer. I don't regret inviting her. She surveys the room with a scowl. "You guys are such cowards. How would you like it if Brandon Sandridge was huddled up at a party with *his* friends blabbering about *you?*"

I sit up and look as dignified as possible, my hands rested one over the other on the outside of my Solo cup. "I, for one, would be honored. Brandon has friends in high places."

Karen turns away. "You're disgusting."

Walker pipes up. "Hey, hey, hey, wait a minute, why are you defending him? It would be one thing if we were picking on some fucking … *Mongoloid* …."

"Oh, my god, did you really just say …?"

He did. Poor word choice, Walker.

"… but this guy is a complete dick. He's a compulsive liar that no one ever called out. When have you *ever* had a positive interaction with him?"

Karen, having said her piece, leaves the room.

Having not finished saying mine, I follow her. Everyone wishes me luck and asks me in passing if I knew that Brandon Sandridge knew about and, in fact, *lives in* the fourth dimension.

Karen did not expect any retaliation and mugs me from behind the beer cooler as I approach. I remember fourth-grade recess with her, our games MacGyvered out of rocks and sticks and climbable plastic structures. Her braces and shoulder freckles. My glasses and *Pokemon* lunch box. Brandon hadn't moved here yet.

She snaps Mr. Shock Top's neck in one torque of the wrist. The sign of a monkey bar alum. "What?" she argues monosyllabically.

"You really think Brandon can't help lying?"

She hyperbolizes a shrug, teetering Shock's corpse within single digits of spilling. "Isn't that obvious?"

"No."

"*OK.*"

It's my turn to pontificate. "You think that he's managed to get this far and achieve *all that he has* with no agency over his interactions with people? That his elaborate web of lies isn't a conscious choice? No ...." I skewer a word from the middle-distance. "A conscious *effort?*" Nice.

"You really want to talk about this in front of all of these people? What if he's here?"

"Would *you* invite him to something like this?"

"No, but ...." Karen sips and backtracks. He probably wouldn't have been able to make it. I'd heard something about a hot date with an old out-of-town acquaintance. "I didn't say his stories were a bad thing. You have your eccentricities."

"You're right, I do, but *yes*, you *did*. You were talking about his compulsive lying like it's a handicap."

"It *is* a handicap!"

"Is it? Or is it a learned habit that he's couched his identity in?"

Karen squints at me. "Do I *know you?*" She lost the braces but kept the shoulder freckles.

My eyes retain their dimensions. "You did." I know this game we play.

Others come to raid the beer chest and we move to the kitchen where a guy is puking in my sink, then move to the laundry room where it smells quieter.

All this walking has moved the conversation forward. "Why do you care?" She frowns with words.

I shrug. "I don't want my achievements cheapened by someone else's counterfeits."

Her eyebrows raise in some neurochemical catalyzation. "You feel threatened. It sounds like you feel *threatened* by Brandon Sandridge." Her breath moves to the back of her throat, sounding similar in execution to a stifled laugh.

I ask about it. "Did you stifle a laugh just then?"

"When?"

"Just then."

"No?"

"When you said his name you said it like it was something to be ridiculed."

"I didn't, actually. I said it like one would say the name of *Brandon Sandridge*."

I point with my beer hand. "You just did it again!" She shakes her head. "You said it like being threatened by Brandon's ... *Brandon-ness* was something to be ashamed of."

"Is it?"

"Dude, *fuck* no."

"Then why are you being so defensive about it?"

"I'm not! I'm just trying to point out that you're being hypocritical about this." Women three years out of highschool don't like to be called that. I persist. "You're talking about Brandon's like he's something omitted from consideration when you were just railing on us about bringing up his lies—."

"*He's pitiful.*" She drags out that last word like runtime will help its potency. "You're picking on a pitiful little guy that doesn't know any better."

I shake my head. "Not true. OK, so, let me ask you this." The washing machine's response to my seat atop it is a dull *wallah.* "Do you take anything he says seriously?"

She's lost musical chairs and she's being dismissive. "I haven't seen or heard from Brandon since we graduated."

"Whatever, *did* you take anything he *said* seriously?"

She *fucking* shrugs. "Sure! Why not?"

"OK, so, why?"

"Because he's a person? Because why would he lie about everything?"

"I'm just trying to nail down why he gets such a pass for being a liar."

"Because it's a coping mechanism, Devin. Have you really never considered that?"

I scrunch my mouth up. "I have. I just don't think that's good enough."

She's not satisfied. "What *exactly* in your life ... what *personal achievements* of yours have been jeopardized by Brandon's stories? What's *big, strong college baseball boy Devin* got to fear from a guy who peaked in middle school?"

That's what I boil down to, huh?

Myself having peaked in high school and being equipped with no real counter-argument, me give shrug that reflects both items.

She's really good at scoffing. "You're acting like an asshole."

I scratch the end of my nose with my beer hand. "Really?"

Karen scrunches her face inward and moves counterclockwise to eleven o'clock. "Really. You have been since freshman year."

"Of college?"

"High school, Devin. I didn't go to college."

In that pause I know I'm going to fuck it up.

"You were cuter with braces."

Another bullseye scoff. "You know, I never really took you for the bully type, *Devin*." She says my name softly, like a well-aimed insult. She walks away and I let her. I don't feel like I've won anything. I don't tell her about being one of Brandon's first friends. I don't tell her how hard it was for me to cave.

I wait a minute and then rejoin the party.

Did you hear about the time Brandon Sandridge graduated from college debt-free a year early and used the extra money to take a Caribbean cruise?

Remember when Brandon Sandridge won some local book awards for opening up about the trials of his compulsive disorder and talked at length about the catharsis he felt using his impediment to empower others like him?

I heard that he's gone East and started doing cybersecurity for some big tech firm where he works in a big server room with no windows and listens to mash-up music.

My sister told me she saw his wedding announcement on Facebook and that he married someone non-binary and has plans to grow out his hair and adopt.

Someone told me he's happy.

Someone told me Brandon Sandridge ended up happy.

That one I can't say straight-faced.

David Herghelegiu

The First Baptist, the Last Amen

I stoned the baptist in myself
and heard my great-grandfather's weeping.
An echo from Romania, when his neighbors tied
him to a horse, taunting his newfound religion
as they spat curses of damnation. The cracking
of his bones rang as they dragged him to the river,
threw him in, so the water would choke out
his prayers. He was saved by shepherds from a nearby hill
who pulled him out as he said *Amen.*

I stoned the baptist in myself
with a handful of pills. I whispered my last
amen and choked on vomit. Sank into
the floorboard, into the hospital mattress where
I awoke after doctors pumped the prayer out
of my system. My mother held my hand between hers,
trying to understand why. As we drove home
I let the pastor on the radio answer for me,
Homosexuality is a direct path to hell.

Samuel J Adams

The Roving Clap'n'Taps' Farewell Show

SPONTANEOUS COMBUSTION

Twenty years ago, Buster Perkins gave his daughter and fellow puppeteer, Zora, a photocopied printout about spontaneous combustion. He'd gotten the article from an obscure journal of Victorian Studies whose name he could not now remember, the sort of publication librarians sent him to after he hassled them for insights relevant to his work. His medium was jig dolls, little wooden figures with spinning arms and hinged legs the puppeteer beat against a springboard for music, and these English creations were popular in the nineteenth century. The monochromatic picture in the center of the article was hard to understand without a caption, but after a few seconds its meaning became clear. Where people once had been, heaps of ashes, hats, and shoes now lay: whitish grit dirtying dark brick ground.

He brought the printout to Zora with her breakfast. She was sitting on a vinyl deck chair on the bean-shaped concrete patio in the small yard of their home in Vacaville, California. She wore neon-striped leggings, scarlet-tinted hair, and a Guns N' Roses T-shirt with its collar slit to increase the view of cleavage. It was 11 a.m.—90 degrees already with the hazy air motionless over the yellowing grass—and Zora was drunk.

"Says here ...," Buster said, tapping the page. "What it says is ... the Victorians had it that liquor increases your risk for spontaneous combustion."

Zora raised a King Cobra bottle to lips still purply with last night's wine and clunked it emptily on the curb beside her.

"That doesn't sound very spontaneous to me," Zora said, looking at the picture.

"Zora ...," Buster said, not knowing what else to say. "Won't no good come of ...."

Zora interrupted him by flicking her Bic lighter and bringing the flame under her chin. She cackled until her father went back inside and slid the glass door quietly behind him.

This happened many years before Zora's drinking was to Buster and others a foregone and despairing conclusion, and although this memory did not indicate any real low yet hit in his daughter's relationship with him or her liquor, Buster thought about it more often than other telling moments in their life together.

It was one of the memories that came to Buster in the Chowchilla County fairgrounds as he sat in a fold-out chair next to his truck and enjoyed the view of a moonlit Ferris wheel and eating a bowl of homemade gazpacho the night before Zora died.

ZORA AWAKENS

To a puppeteer, the world avails a potentiality of puppets. Shoes, socks, silverware, gin bottles, dry leaves, stones, beer cans, books, the packaging of Snackables, scratched lotto tickets, bottle caps, felt-tip pens—everything applies, everything has its use.

Awaken with the detritus of any unkempt bedroom swirled around you, slip off your bed, and begin to comb the floor: If it takes you more than thirty seconds to find a suitable object and pair it with a convincing vocal style, a traceable story, and a unique bearing with which it moves through the physical world, then you are no puppeteer. And if you awaken to a clean floor, you are a puppeteer unlike any Zora Perkins had met in her forty-four years as a puppeteer's daughter and her twenty-four puppeteering and music-making with her dad in The Roving Clap'n'Taps.

Zora came to in her trailer and watched the mottled dustiness swirl around her: tiny angels of her private pollution. Ashtrays overflowed, green mites scaled down spider plants, and Zora's pores crackled with yesterday's dirt. Central Valley sunlight spangled the woodwork and crept under the curtains, cooked the metal edges where the windows rested, and blurred the room in a portentous orange glare in which the red dots of the digital clock eventually aligned to say 7:30, an unsurprising number that nevertheless made Zora groan.

The Roving Clap'n'Taps were performing in five hours.

BUSTER AWAKENS

Buster Perkins woke at quarter to eight in the slide-in trailer attached to the bed of his '97 Silverado. He'd slept beneath one satin sheet and atop eight expensive Navajo blankets he had collected over years touring the west. He wore his only sleepwear, an oversized T-shirt and long johns, both turned by time and travel the graying color of moth cocoons. Buster tried to keep things light and spartan in the slide-in, as he devoted most of his truck's towing capacity to Zora's trailer and to his chest of wooden bandmates, the jig dolls. Now seventy, Buster had been a professional puppeteer for forty-two years and he hadn't touched a marionette in forty, and some days he couldn't tell which fact made him prouder. Jig dolls settled nicely onto the chip against artistic snobbery Buster carried on his shoulder.

Buster pulled his Silverbelly Stetson hat off a mannequin head, waxed and twisted his handlebar mustache to the fullest exaggerated width, and commenced snapping together the fastens of his paisley-print shirt. He grabbed his jeans from the mini-freezer and beat the frost from the crotch, then brewed coffee and poured it into a castellated pewter stein. Then he opened the chest where the puppets slept and looked upon his little loves.

His jig dolls stood six inches tall. Their forms were hewn from wood with little regard for verisimilitude: Some heads were persimmon-shaped, some segmented like Tootsie Rolls. Their faces were painted on in broad, smiley strokes. Their suits and dresses were painted in uniform color with pointillist dots for buttons and crudely daubed stripes for sleeves. The dolls' legs hung on loosely and were jointed at the knees, and their hinged arms spun and dangled. The puppeteer held sticks that skewered their middles and extended six inches from their backs, and, wielded with skill, the sticks summoned the puppets' slack limbs into graceless dances, sodden slouches, nimble flips, clownish falls, all while the dolls' feet clattered musically on a vibrating oak springboard held by the puppeteer's other hand. The dolls kept time as needed, clomped a 6/8 jig or leisurely tapped a 3/4 waltz. They didn't make great music, but when good music was played, the clacking of jig doll feet added an interesting castanet beat: a polyrhythmic clogging manageable even by the drunken hands of Zora Perkins. She'd been slipping off-beat lately but still recovered whenever Buster shot her a concerned look from across the stage.

Buster figured that to an unlearned audience watching the shows, any off-beat mistakes would be easily attributable to the rank stupidity of the flopping puppet instead of the soggy untethering of everything in his daughter that had been holding her together. He wondered if that was too cynical a line of thought for his mind to take and then reflected that like most brutal insights concerning Zora, it had probably originated with her. Most people Buster knew with a strong grasp on self-awareness never got much use from it, and Zora, exceptional in many ways, was no exception in this.

His truck and Zora's attached trailer were parked in a part of the lot marked for the Chowchilla County Fair's "traveling talent." Buster looked out across the lot and watched the day-workers arriving, Civics and Altimas packed shoulder to shoulder with teenagers ready to hawk elephant ears or pick up garbage with grappling wands or blow leaves about with leaf blowers. Kids in their parents' cars, earning money for clothes and summer fun, accelerating toward adulthood at varying degrees of heedlessness. The cars squeaked into their spots, and the people that came out of them looked young, recoverable, shiny.

"Time to rise, Zora," Buster yelled, lofting the words out like a shot put aimed directly for the roof of his daughter's Scamp trailer. And since words were sometimes not enough to wake her, he picked up a stone and chucked that at her roof, too.

ZORA AND THE JAR OF PICKLES

Zora heard her father's yell and felt, like a headache, the stone thud her roof. She slipped from her bed, slipped a baggy Voodoo Lounge Tour T-shirt over her pajama bottoms, kicked the floor's dirty clothes toward their proper pile, and grabbed a jar of jumbo pickles from a shelf. She centered the jar upon a fold-out Formica table that—because of her father's errant attempts at welding and soldering—no longer quite folded in. She exhaled loudly through her nostrils; a nose hair fluttered and she plucked it, tear ducts tingling, eyes still crisped with the grit of sleep. She had become a large woman, staying fat even on days when food was skipped entirely for beer, and it had become a humiliating business to get her legs under the table, which demanded intimate knee-to-table snugness even of slim people and set Zora's swelling knees in a punitive brace. She put her hands on the tabletop, and squished her thighs in laterally, the hinged parts of her popping audibly in the process. The table brayed about its misuse in the place where it joined the wall. Percussed by this jostling, the six green, dimpled occupants of the pickle jar bobbed and swayed. Zora opened the lid, and let the trailer fill with the jar's briny smell, a djinn of vinegar to grant her wishes. Of all olfactory camouflages, pickles worked best. *Nobody trusts the smell of mouthwash after noon*, as Buster put it years ago, after the time of fatherly pleas for temperance had passed.

She could have smelled openly of her bibulous faults if she didn't work such a childish circuit. But at the wholesome fairgrounds and farmers' markets where the Roving Clap'n'Taps roved, a boozy odor was forever banned while the smell of pickles was forever welcomed, the forty-sixth star in the flag of summertime scents America waved at the noses of her people. The jar of bobbing pickles began sliding leftward, and Zora wondered if Buster hadn't done one of his favorite nighttime tricks, hitching her trailer to his truck and parking it on the sheerest available slant. Her father had abandoned most pranks but not this. He used it to undermine her goals for perpetual lounging. Then Zora remembered how flat Chowchilla was and figured she'd just nudged the jar.

She looked through the yellowy glass and watched a pickle slowly turn to show dimples mistakable for a mouth and a face. She removed this smiley standout and set him upon a napkin.

"Still feeling a little pickled yourself, eh Zor-Zor?" the pickle said to her through the twangy voice she gave it. She rolled its head back and forth reproachfully.

Something glinted from under the curtains, and when Zora parted them she saw a Taaka vodka bottle slanted sidewise against the glass. Whether she'd hidden it from guests or herself didn't matter: The vodka's sickly warmth felt nice sloshing down her. It carried the appeal of a bag of French fries a stoned, hungry high-schooler might find on a car's warm floormat and happily consume knowing that nothing so inherently unhealthy could possibly despoil.

"You up yet?" Buster yelled.

"Yeah!" she shouted.

"Sorry, pal," she told Petey the pickle before setting in her dentures and decapitating his green head.

BUSTER SHOOTS OUT THE CLOWN TEETH

Buster understood his daughter well enough to know that once she woke up, any attempts to hasten her morning routine would only lengthen it, make it noisier, and have it subtly worm into his routine until it, too, was ruined. He decided to kill time by walking into the fairgrounds and shooting out some piano-key clown teeth before the fairgoers began their frenzied whirl through the turnstiles. Even at eight-thirty in early May, the day already threatened disgusting heat. The low, cool, thick tule fog that often settles upon Chowchilla and makes the San Joaquin valley seem livable by disappearing miles of its flat, unsettled embarrassments and it bespoke either a great will or a fierce intractability that Zora could sleep in on days like this. She'd been the same or worse at waking up starting in middle school and on through her alternately manic and slumberous teenaged years. Whenever Buster tried blasting fuzzed radios or doing the cold-washcloth-on-the-face trick, such stratagems brought on only teary fights, the destruction of his property, and phoned explanations from him about why Zora was once again arriving ten minutes late into her second class of the day.

From a drink stand that opened early, Buster bought an Arnold Palmer, virgin. Zora came by her day-drinking afflictions naturally— maternal genes and friends' gifts—but not through him. Good things came to her naturally, too: a fierce intelligence and gift for music. Matters would have been simpler if drinking were Zora's only area of precocity. But in school Zora tested well enough for her teachers to overlook tardiness and absences, well enough to impress, hearten, and eventually pain her father. On her sixteenth birthday, she took the GED along with a bunch of friends after a pre-planned motel bender underwritten by a great-aunt's check. After two months of her hanging around the house, Buster paid for her SATs. She killed the test well enough for the Perkins' mailbox to swell with brochures from hoity-toity schools Buster knew had the means to subsidize the education of the low-income daughter of an uneducated, single-parent puppeteer. But to Zora the point of testing well was to test out altogether. Smart as she was, she figured she'd find something to do, and attempts to sway her to another opinion just made her mean. Now, decades later, she still gloated the words, "798 verbal, drunk as fuck," after solving in minutes the crossword puzzle Buster had left rumpled and abandoned. Buster still rued how easy it would have been to just forge some signatures and apply to the schools for her.

The clown teeth game was staffed by a young man in a beanie named Lou. Lou had caught Buster and Zora's act yesterday and liked what he saw well enough to watch it through the whole of his stoned lunch break. "Great shit," he'd said. "You make those guys yourself?" Zora had ignored Lou and made a beeline straight for the nectar in her trailer, but Buster affirmed that he'd made many such puppets and began the highlights of his stump speech on his expertise, hitting the major points—how jig dolls didn't have overhead strings or need them; how no spidery French-ified subtlety lay behind their rude poetry, only the authentic clunk of wood; how, in the classic design, the bodies and heads don't move, and only the limbs swung and danced. Maybe that's not much movement, Buster admitted, but the shadow puppets of Java didn't move much, either, and these were considered— by more than just puppet enthusiasts, mind you—among the artistic wonders of human creation. Above all, Buster stressed that jig dolls were an underdog art: paupers' toys that had their historical heyday in the grubbier quarters of London, built cheap but built to last (a few troupe members in his chest had reached centenarian status and wore their many years better than he or Zora). Throughout this speech, Lou had nodded in a wide-eyed, continuous way Buster enjoyed. "Crazy things, man," Lou said. "Who knew? Well, I know it's not much, but you can come by the booth and shoot free."

But it was much. Knowing the guy who controls the clown teeth was the sort of thing that counted as a perk of fairgrounds living, a victory. Buster told Lou good morning, picked up the bright green gun and shot the teeth out, ten for ten. Even though it was an hour before the paying public breached the turnstiles, Lou let Buster pick his animal. He considered a pink elephant too on-the-nose for his alcoholic, forty-something daughter, so he got a wearable, stuffed sloth that hugged its sewn-together arms around one's neck like a tired, mangy infant. But it wasn't a real infant, so Buster felt no qualms at all walking out the staff exit from the fairgrounds with a lit cigarette dangling from his mouth, dropping ashes on the plush fur cozied about him, looking with hedged hopes at the mists effulging from Zora's trailer.

ZORA TAKES A SHOWER

In the last shower she would ever take, Zora washed herself with the sea-salt gypsy hand soap she'd bought at the fair the day before. The salt stung little tears in her as she squeaked bubbles along her body's paler reaches, and she made mental notes of places to daub with rubbing alcohol when she got out. Cuts healed slowly now, incompletely. As a child, she had scraped her knees with the best of the block, but she'd avoided external injuries most of her adulthood. Now it was as if she had entered life's second phase of Band-Aid use, one only the infirm and unsteady know. When she lifted her elbow, the spray washed off a browning zebra-striped bandage and spun it lazily around the drain. At forty-two, Zora accepted the ridiculousness of bodies as the case of the world: She'd lived long enough and hard enough to know a body didn't require man-sized marionette strings and the pulling capacities of a yard crane to be yanked independently of its wishes, to topple over and then stagger up pathetically to collect the crowd's reluctant sympathies. And what was true of a body was truer still of its parts—toes, noses, whole limbs went and puppetized themselves quite independently of one's will. She eyed her hands under the pounding water, her right ring finger and pinky wiggling involuntarily, a dance they'd been doing for near-on half a decade. The digits moved like blown-up pictures of Petri-dish specimens, those little, essential cells whose jerky movements on a projector screen had persuaded a teenaged, psilocybin-addled Zora that puppetry had a determinative hold on all things, that it went on this way inside and out, tugging every eyelet in the whole, goddamned great chain of being. And she knew a great string-pulling was nigh. *Wernicke-Korsakoff. Cirrhosis. Arrhythmia.* Things she couldn't spell were coming to kill her, and she'd been such a good speller.

By the time the water cooled, she'd emptied a Coors tall can and halved a bottle of Seagram's. Getting out, she remembered to disguise her breath for the upcoming performance with her dad by eating a pickle.

BUSTER'S PRACTICE

Buster heard with relief the muted rustlings, bumps, and throat-clearings that announced the formation of his daughter's day coming from her trailer, and he began setting out the jig dolls needed for the performance upon a fold-out table.

Standing over the crew in a Stetson that would have looked statelier had the feather in its band not shed every plume, Buster resembled a sheriff pep-talking his motley unit before a standoff. It was, in its way, a diverse group: Dapper Dan and Steppin' Sam were black, Agatha the Witch was green, and Big Mean Lee (a custom piece wrought in cedar) was a badger in overalls. Buster took out a Jumpin' Jill from 1922, set it on a springboard, and started to loosen his wrist with a beat. He sang an old tune—*I don't like a railroad man, a railroad man gonna kill you if he can*—which, in deference to model-train enthusiasts and railroad employees, Buster avoided singing on county-fair stages.

It wasn't always fairs and schools. They'd played plenty of clubs, and occasionally Buster's puppeteering chops and his penchant for soft-spoken grandstanding about his expertise in Moose lodges and barrooms had earned him other perks: guest lecture gigs at art academies, panel seats at folkloric conferences, a few cuts on an album of outsider Americana, some session work clogging doll feet on German-produced zydeco tunes. Sometimes the sophisticated world blended with his own, and he didn't exactly mind. He set down Jumpin' Jill and began to ready a breakfast for him and his daughter. He cracked eggs over an outdoor skillet and cooked, and above him particulates of dirtied air danced palpably as the heat upon Chowchilla's dusty flatness began returning itself upwards, back to the sun.

AS IF FROM A CUCKOO CLOCK

Zora emerged from her trailer holding Troll-o-lol, a frizzy-haired custom piece Buster had made for her tenth birthday, and the one water bottle she had that she still exclusively filled with water. She was still in her pajamas, far from ready, but he appreciated her making an appearance, popping out like the figure in a cuckoo clock does to demonstrate time is working.

"Morning, Pop," she said before a fit of coughing took her. She motioned him over and handed him Troll-o-lol, a gesture of collateral to prove she was on her way to joining the world. She'd brandished it in earnest in middle school and used it as a bitter in-joke between them now.

Buster was still wearing the sloth. "What's that hanging on your shoulder?" said Zora. "My mascot?"

"A sloth. You can hold her when you come out and ... join the living," Buster said.

"You didn't soak those things in wood polish again, did you?" Zora said, looking at the puppets. "That goo makes my head spin."

"Well, wouldn't that be tragic," Buster said.

Zora spun back into the trailer, spun out again minutes later in a cowboy shirt and jeans.

"I'm gonna go around, gather us up some coffee," Zora said. Buster tilted his Stetson and cast an inspecting eye her way. "I know," Zora said. "*No more Chicos.* I'll behave. They got a Dutch Bros knock-off. Holland Hermanos, something like that. I wanted to see it."

"Ain't no way that's the name," Buster said, chuckling quietly.

CHICO

Buster didn't know the proper names for Zora's failing health, but such particulars were not essential to understand things were worsening and that any day could be the one or could point at the one. Two months ago, in Chico, he'd found her in her trailer, irrecoverable from her drooling slouch, too soused to perform. Upon discovering her so, he called the bookers and spun a tale of food poisoning that he imagined earned a few knowing eyerolls. When, hours later, his daughter looked greened and unimproved, she assented to go to the urgent care place. A nurse guided Zora to a room where they made her drink a charcoal shake to neutralize her liver. It wasn't her first time drinking the stuff, but she vomited like it was, as anyone will. She slept nine hours in her trailer then left for the store. She returned with ruffled chips and two bottles of chardonnay clinking around in a plastic bag. Buster sighed at the sound of what moderation meant to her.

The next morning, he spoke the only ultimatum he'd tried in a while. "Now, listen ... what happened ... well ... there can't be any more days like that. For the band's sake." The money the Roving Clap'n'Taps made was never lucrative but always necessary. Cancellations got them nothing.

"And for my sake?" she asked, head in her pillow. "Can I rest in this Western oasis?"

"You work three-hour days and sleep ten," he'd told her. "Any more downtime than that'd kill you … you know that better than me."

"Freaking Svengali over here," Zora said.

"Yeah … right … him."

MOCHAS

Zora walked toward the fairground gate, turned left at a lawn where young men were picking up trash with grappling wands, passed taco trucks, smoothie stands, and the gear-twirling barkers of kettle corn—the people of the world pulling and heaving in dollar-made movement. Then a single-file line of folks passed her, displaying movements that came from other forces: They had palsies; spasms; crutches; kindly, elderly aides who walked beside them. It was the fair's "Special Friends Day," and the friends were capitalizing on their free admission.

From the line, a young man with soft cobalt eyes faced her. He had a pleasant if gnashing face that reminded her of Eric, a former fling. Eric had been a habitual over-consumer of Zora's Adderall, and the pills did a number on his neurology: Forty milligrams in and his face gnawed and snapped and chewed the air. The gesture brought mortification to adults and giggly delight to the high-school buddies who nicknamed him "Pac-Man." Zora could remember watching in bafflement as Eric stood before a mirror, taking long, mindful breaths to control the movements, and failed to do any more than limit the frequency of the visibly painful chomps; no matter what Eric wanted his mouth to do, his mouth just wanted to keep on eating dots. Last Zora heard, Eric had reformed of these habits, relocated to Idaho. His fairground doppelganger wore a flannel tied around his waist and maintained a great stride to stay beside his staff in the front of the line. A small, wrinkly woman in a wide-brimmed sun cap cawed requests for Dr. Pepper, and a blind fellow behind her tapped his cane and held the plushy arm of a large woman. Like butterflies reaching fore-ordained flowers, the group stopped before the bright colors of a lemonade-and-pretzel stand.

At Der Windmill Coffees, Zora bought two large iced mochas with whipped cream and stepped beneath an umbrella table's shade to Irish one with a flask. A Hispanic kid in an event staff T-shirt paused his desultory sweeping to watch her.

"It's OK," Zora said. "I'm a puppeteer."

"I ain't judging," the kid said.

"An *artiste*." She slurped her straw loudly and walked back toward her trailer.

The heat hitting the hazy blacktop returned to it a smell like the time-dirtied version of its first tarring. Why was the Central Valley so willing to embody everybody's mean jokes about it? Even in May the blacktop got hot enough to fry an egg. Being ovoid and but fragilely intact herself, Zora sizzled with worry when she found her dad and gave him an iceless, overflowing mocha.

BURGERS

His father took the mocha and guzzled it. "They selling burgers, Zor." He was sitting on a curb with Stewart, an elephant ear vendor, a joint aglow between them.

"Who's cooking?" Zora said. "Shriners or Rotary Club? I'm not eating any undercooked crap."

"Firemen. They're passing around the boots for some charity thing … handsome fellers."

Across the lot, navy blue shirts bulged from the chests of the last American men permitted to attractively wear suspenders. Smoke billowed deliciously from their grills.

"Firemen, huh. Well, they should know how to do it."

Stewart the elephant ear vendor giggled about something, his skinny arms shaking at the place his hands disappeared into Carhartt pockets.

"What you laughing at, peewee?" Zora asked.

"You," Stewart said. "*Shriners don't grill burgers right*—that's a funny observation."

"Well, I must have misspoken. Shriners grill burgers *exactly* right. I'd eat a Shriner burger if it had a fez on it. It's the Rotary Club don't know what in the biohazardous fuck they're doing."

Zora brought back a burger with grilled onions and appealingly blackened jalapenos. Somewhere in Dr. Mike Trenton's storm of doomful forecasts for Zora's body had been a contraindication against hot peppers, and two bites into the burger the greasy jalapenos hit her gut like coals in a sauna. A bathroom break would be required. Then aperitifs and pickles. She coughed with ripped, papery breaths and walked into the trailer with her hand on her chest.

"Nice lady, your wife," said Stewart, swaying approvingly.

"She's my daughter," corrected Buster. "But do yourself a favor and back off anyway."

Zora still occasionally took men to her trailer and Vaselined her hand for liquor-acquisition strategies of which Buster did not approve.

ZORA'S WARMUP; ORIGINS OF THE BAND

Back at the trailer, Zora uncased her fiddle, did some pizzicato plucking, and wiggled the tuning pegs. Three fans shuffled around the smells of her and her home. She thought of the trailer as her home: paid off five years before, the last item she could really save for. She could be territorial about her only formidable asset, even toward the man who towed it. She permitted Buster to leave his slide-in for Zora's couch only on the coldest nights, and even then he needed to wear earplugs through Zora's haranguing and her snores. For all the time they spent together, it was important for Zora—and for Buster—to believe that Zora had become as she was on her own.

In high school, when her Suisun City friends were over, passing a rum bottle and 7 Up chasers up and down the clawfoot couch in Buster's garage, some friend would mention how chill it must be having a guy like Buster for a dad. They were right that the kindly, loping man was refreshingly permissive, but wrong in thinking that this disinclined Zora from rebellion. Even though at 17.99 years old she had every desired freedom granted her, Zora's eighteenth birthday felt to her like a great weight removed. Shaking out rationalizing bits of brain from her ears, she departed their little ranch house to travel the archipelago of couches and lovers' beds all around Solano and Yolo Counties. Her sable hair grew longer, her eyeshadow darkened, her thighs became smoothly tuberous as they were petted and gripped by the boys of Vacaville, Winters, West Sacramento, and beyond. Zora spent two years turbulent with liberty, besotted with drink, motoring on pills, buoyed aloft on the loose bills of her indulgers and the beer-and-pizza cash she earned busking downtown Davis or Old Sac, trotting out Troll-o-lol and other jig dolls her father had packed in her duffel after realizing he couldn't persuade her to stay. But in time the boys ignored her, couches forbade her, summertime heat and parking tickets made her Corolla unlivable. After months of detachment punctuated only by stray phone calls and occasional brunches together, she arrived at Buster's door, asking to stay. Buster gave her a hug not quite as long as the hug she needed and began moving his tinker-table and puppet-making implements from her room to the garage. Neither one said anything big that night: No shows were booked, no vows announced, and Buster tuckered out early listening to Zora play her chiming twelve-string. The troupe wouldn't form for four months, wouldn't perform for six. But both daughter and father agreed the Roving Clap'n'Taps started with Zora's return, that the jig dolls in Buster's chest smiled happily about their future uses ....

Zora was playing a sprightly melody of Brahms from her fully tuned fiddle when her father knocked on the door.

"On in thirty, Zora ...."

Zora ceased fiddling, said OK, and remembered the Maker's Mark in her cabinet.

WHAT ZORA WANTS

... is not exactly to die, not precisely to live, and most emphatically to drink, Drink, DRINK. Let inspirational strings chime through other fiddles, not hers; her lips will never form a prayer of any thanks, a renunciation of any sincerity. When she goes, she hopes it's quick, not too rough for her dad. And if Buster could open her brain, she hopes those thoughts and concerns run like the chyron on the news channels Buster so avidly watched on rare nights they splurged on motels. She'd never wanted to hurt him. Even hurting herself had been, at most, an afterthought.

SHOW PREP

Sun-bronzed the crowds came, from all over Madera and Fresno Counties, up highways running to Tulare and Pixley, passing cotton fields, nut orchards, correctional facilities, ditches full of crow-pecked refuse, and water towers whose dusted exteriors monumentalized dryness. People didn't attend the fair for puppet shows, and yet seeking tented reprise from the heat—and the noise, the costly rides whose metal surfaces singed fingertips, the stinky bustle at the replacement heifers' competition, the overpriced pretzels sold so salty you bought the overpriced lemonade, too—the people found their way to the puppets.

As Buster tilted mics on the stage to lap height, he wondered if the extent of the Roving Clap'n'Taps fandom might more honestly reveal itself in more temperate climes, when they weren't on a double bill with free shade and ample benches. But their business peaked as spring turned to summer—pepper-picking season—when the fairs were up and parks held outdoor concerts and the kids were out of school. It used to be the season Buster saved up to put his daughter through treatment, and he'd conclude it by driving her trailer up to some restful, lakeside setting. But over the years he learned repose endangered her more than stress. Work, alone, sustained Zora, and Zora always appreciated the work.

Zora took up the fiddle and did top-forty melodies through the sound check, getting laughs with "I Can't Feel My Face When I'm With You." Buster stepped up to her to ask if she was ready and smelled her pickle breath with satisfaction when she said yes. Buster picked up his springboard and his Steppin' Sam jig doll. Steppin' Sam, Buster's oldest authentic piece, was a black man outfitted in red like a bellhop, and, in keeping with the times, Buster threw Sam's voice with less gravelly soul than he used to. Buster and his jig doll bowed to the crowd, and Buster began his introductory speech.

LADIES AND GENTLEMEN, THE ROVING CLAP'N'TAPS!

"Ladies and gentlemen, little folk and large, friends, Romans, countrymen ... we are the Roving Clap'n'Taps, the only ten-member band in America that's eighty-percent wood. I'm Buster Perkins, this is my daughter Zora on fiddle, and this here's Steppin' Sam on percussion. You ready to groove, Sam?

"Groove? Man, I'm a hundred years old.'"

"That mean you were born ready?"

"NO, it means I was carved a hundred years ago from a block of wood."

"Well, you played fine yesterday."

"I was only ninety-nine then."

"Oh, so now that you're a hundred, it's different?"

"Yeah. Wooden teeth can't chomp down no food but cream corn."

"Did you say, 'green corn'?"

And at the utterance of "green corn," Zora's fiddle blares into the old Leadbelly tune, Buster chugs out the lyric (*Green corn, come along, Cholly*), and Steppin' Sam begins his prancing polyrhythms. Three verses in, Zora takes over singing duties so Steppin' Sam can protest about having his corn commentary misheard. When the song ends,

Steppin' Sam begins a rant about the mistreatment of the elderly, then Zora chases him offstage using Django the Dragon, a large, green, custom-made piece with hinged, oaken mandibles. She sets Django on her springboard, and Buster picks up his Martin Dreadnought and begins strumming a bluegrass-y version of "Puff the Magic Dragon." The crowd ceases their squirmy inattention; giggles ascend up grade levels, first the manically overdone laughs of preschoolers, then the knowing tittering of seven-year-olds, and, finally, the charmed chuckle of tweens and special-needs adults that fall on Zora and Django. Buster watches the musical mists of Hohnalee fill with such innocent faces, and he feels that old performative thrill that makes him tally his deeds as they should be tallied; a misinterpreted life is not a life misspent, especially with these crowds. And because the crowd today seems especially large, their faces especially warm, Buster plays so merrily that the chords keep coming seconds after Zora topples from her chair and her dragon skitters across the stage, snapping at its stick. Buster drops his guitar, runs to Zora, cups her head in his hand, and shouts for an ambulance in a heightened, broken voice that seems to belong to someone else. Buster looks into the crowd's confused, frightened eyes, sees pupils dart away like tadpoles eluding ripples in a pond

ZORA ON THE GURNEY

Zora came to on the gurney, the ambulance knocking about in a rush to Chowchilla Medical Center; it wasn't her first time waking in one, but the novelty of it felt fresh. Two men in blue sat near her with Buster beside them. Buster regarded her with a considerate lean, shading her from the shrieking-bright paneling with the cool dome of his hat brim. Her eyelids twitched. Her father leaned over, poured water into his palm and touched it to her forehead as if the heat he sensed rising within her was within his power to assuage, and the paramedics humored his awkward ministrations. From Zora's forehead, cheeks, and neck, thick beads of sweat rolled nowhere and felt chilly where they stalled. Buster's wide-brimmed head swayed like a mobile piece above her, and a slow, plodding tear dripped from his left eye; she'd forgotten he only wept from one eye.

The paramedics trundled her out the vehicle and pushed her through the ER's slow-to-part automated doors.

THE ER

In the entryway, Zora and Buster separated so Buster could handle the intake paperwork. When he finished, the woman at the desk gave him a room number but said Zora wouldn't be able to talk right away. Were there other family members to contact? "Some cousins, but I'll take care of it," Buster said before striding down the hall.

"Sir. She cannot yet be seen."

Buster turned and sat down and waited for what seemed a very long time.

ZORA's ROOM

The woman at the desk addressed Buster as "sir" again and pointed him toward someone else. "This is Fan. You'll want to follow him."

The short, slick-haired man was already moving down the hallway, so Buster followed.

Down the corridor, people were sitting on benches—faces slouched and bleared with inconveniences were held with cupped hands—or looking askance at the diverting sight of the tall, lugubriously striding cowboy with a broken hat feather. Buster looked down into the marbled smear of the linoleum and felt haunted: There was light hovering above this floor that seemed to come not from the rectangular light fixtures but the sun blazing beyond the walls, the force that makes tomatoes plump and makes raisins of the valley's people, who fill up the region's dreary hospitals suffering from conditions that seemed preventable until the very day they became inevitable. He'd raised Zora in the milder north until debts pushed them south, shoved them down I-99 like a chute. The sun wasn't always the culprit in the crimes against the people of the valley, but that high and angry orb was always, at some level, an accomplice. North of the valley, people tanned; here, they crackled, ossified, eroded. Even May could turn you, after April had her chances.

"Zor-ah Perkins," Fan said after Buster caught up with him. "Room 107."

Zora lay on a tilted bed, neck and shoulder hunched to the left. Her mouth slacked open and the part of her lip she'd bitten when she fell drooped heavily and had a bloom of purple. Her body looked like it had been heaped there in haste. Cords ran from her, drips on four-legged IV poles. The cords looked strong enough to lift her, and

Buster winced at the thought of gauze unsticking, needles ripping out, wheeled poles toppling, tethers tangling and failing his daughter.

"Can I … uh … straighten her out?" Buster asked. "I don't know why they put her leaning all … catawampus like this."

Fan stepped into the hall and looked around. "Yes. Go ahead."

Buster budged her into place and tucked up her blankets. Fan said a doctor would be in soon and then he left.

Zora's jaundiced skin looked yellower and looser. Slivers of conquering gray shimmered like tinsel in her raven-dark hair. The ventilator was running, and Buster couldn't identify which breathing noises were hers as he watched the accordion-patterned plastic rise and fall. The room was full of the smell he'd urged Zora to rectify in what now seemed too-gentle terms, a swampy scent of the inner world where the booze traveled. He thought of her liver, pictured it puffing through her skin like the puffer of a bullfrog.

From a nearly empty green Kleenex box on an end table, Buster took the last wad of tissue and daubed his eye. He sat on a wheeled chair and shut his eyes for a minute, listening to clocks tick and the casters of carts swishing down the hallway. Then he got up and rubbed Zora's shoulder. He patted it and pinched it and held it tightly. And then he remembered.

What he remembered was not Zora but the little he had been able to give her. He remembered their work, their only genuine hobby, their only reliable distraction through dark times, the jig dolls who looked upon them with painted eyes of ageless simplicity. Remembered, in the vague, slurred, vaunting diction of his daughter's voice, how in all things lay immanent the capacity to shake to life under sound hands. Remembered how Zora's hands—trembly, arthritic—had honored the puppeteer's pedigree right up until the minute she could no longer use them.

Buster took out his pocketknife, serrated the bottom of the Kleenex box, and folded it inward. He cut eyeholes and a jagged line of teeth, removed a Sharpie from his breast pocket, and soon had a friendly crocodile named Chauncy hanging from his talking hand. Quickly, a story came to Buster: of a sunny world where creatures all glimmeringly wet and happily muddied gathered at the riverbank for conversation. Chauncy Crocodile was gossiping about the foolhardy ways of water buffaloes when Doctor Corazon-Jiménez arrived at room 107. The doctor paused at the entryway and watched as a large, motionless, bedridden woman and a tall, old cowboy with a mangled Kleenex box on his hand performed the Roving Clap'n'Taps' farewell show.

Kathleen Hellen

Wonderboy

You can call me "little shit," as in "little shit,
get your ass over here." I got them stripes to show for it,
like Tony Tiger. Black whip, the TV cable. Miss
Irene holds my shoulders straight and says that sody-
water rots my teeth, but I like Mountain Dew, I like potato chips.
I like the way baloney spits, fried up in the skillet. She says,
"Never leave the baby on the dryer." "Never leave a cigarette."
She says next time she comes, she'll bring Harry Potter.
She says I'm something else—a "slice of wonder," like the bread.

Jonathan Greenhause

Longevity

Start with a dying leaf, which seems healthy. Notice how green it is.
Remark how it carries all the characteristics of longevity.

See its bending stem attached to a small branch, which in turn
is attached to a larger one. Be patient. This is going somewhere.

Now observe how in the photo, Emily's hanging from a larger
    branch,
& she's smiling. She appears to be healthy,

carries all the characteristics of longevity. Observe her clear skin,
the glint in her eyes, the vitality. You wish you could embrace her,

but this picture's from twenty years ago, & now you're approaching
    forty.
Look what happens at its edges, arms clinging

to the large branch holding the smaller one, which holds the stem,
which holds the leaf. When you get the phone call, it's Emily.

But it isn't Emily calling you. It's *about* her. She's let go.
& she can't tell you how to feel or what her death should mean. Just

start with a dying leaf, which seems healthy.
Notice how you don't realize life's slipping away, not until it's fallen.

Jonathan Greenhause

Getting Organized

My indispensable coworker calls out sick
ten times before showing up
for his first day of work. We shoulder the burden
of his absence, perform
voodoo, damn his immortal soul
to make ourselves feel better. It doesn't

rain here very often. We dig holes in the dirt
on our lunch hour. We do it
for fun. Our coworker stays at home
& writes metrical poetry about
the Metric System
vs. Godzilla. We've never really been fans

of venture capitalism. "Occupy Wall Street"
occupied a small park
close to Wall Street. From our tinted windows,
we could see its tents, its signs,
its expression of hope
steadily evaporating. Our weary coworker

calls out sick again. He swears he's got
a mysterious ailment,
fearing work. We're afraid
the globalized world will swallow us whole,
will make us its slaves,
will force us to write our poems in meter.

Amanda Marbais

Tell Me

Greg is telling that story again at the office party, the one where our spokesdog, Biscuit, awakens her owner with a tug to the sleeve before the ceiling collapses in flames. The sales associates have stopped flirting and have abandoned a ransacked snack table. They sip wine from Solo cups and fold their arms across company golf shirts. They appear a little awed, even as their dogs roam the crowd, sniffing paper plates, hands, and occasionally thighs.

"We would have gone bankrupt without that dog," says Greg. His sport jacket and tight jeans shave off ten years, but lately he looks like he came off a bender. His skin is gray and slack.

"It's true." His business partner, Joe, has worn that same red fleece all week, and his tape measure has worn a hole in the back pocket.

"My mom thinks I work for that pet franchise with the dog from *The Today Show*," says a team lead. "Are you saying Biscuit didn't do any of that?"

Andrew, the regional manager, is engrossed in his phone. My phone buzzes with his text. It reads simply, *The Today Show*.

"Plenty of dogs save their owners," says Greg. "They run through fires, pull children from lakes."

"Now, don't bullshit them." Joe laughs. "That dog didn't save anyone." He points to the banner overhead. It has an image of Biscuit, a lab with huge, wet eyes. "She was afraid of thunder."

"Hey. Who knows what that dog has gone on to do," says Greg.

Several sales associates exchange looks. Some laugh. But, it's that *umph* laugh, like heartburn or acknowledging a pun.

"And in two weeks we'll open our third store." Greg starts clapping. Everyone joins him, and the dogs get whipped up and cut the tension with explosive barks.

Was it convivial? Yes. Did it feel like we were a big work-family? It did.

Greg catches my eye as I refill my chardonnay. Maybe he's actually sick and not hungover. I am about to walk over and offer Ibuprofen and Emergen-C from my purse, but he points at my face, his thumb and forefinger forming a gun, and pulls the trigger. He smirks. So I force a smile.

If you suspected your boss to be a criminal, like most people you would call your mom. My mom died when I was young. Pancreatic cancer. This is far lonelier than I let on to friends. You need family, one person who has your back because they've known you since childhood.

Without my mom, that someone is my brother, Elliot. But we only talk once a year. He is a cop who loves jawing about his job, so he squeezes all his stories into one call. He never seems to want to hang up. During our last conversation, he detailed a swatting: twelve officers surrounding a guy's house, creeping along the hydrangea, aiming at this guy's open windows. Officers took cover behind squad cars. Elliot described the sobering feel of leveling a .45 on a man. He corrects himself. "A drug dealer. This was a vendetta swatting."

My brother possesses an unswerving confidence in his own judgment. He is never conflicted. Even his obligatory holiday texts are humblebrags.

Ate too much turkey, time to do a 5K run.

Polished off a bottle of wine last night with a retired senator. Doing a cleanse today.

The whole family hiked ten miles to flat rock. Sprained my ankle. Totally worth it.

Elliot wants to jail all the drug dealers and then the Wall Street crooks. He is a CPA. He plans to work in the financial-crimes division and "catch a Bernie Madoff." I nearly roll my eyes out of my head whenever he says this, but obviously he is the person to call.

Elliot greets me with, "Hey. How ya doing? I'm just starting my weightlifting routine here."

I cut right to it. "I'm pretty sure my boss is embezzling." I explain how Greg has me write huge checks without a single corresponding invoice. Essentially, he just takes out money whenever he feels like it. He *claims* he's buying products COD. When I emailed both Greg and

Joe, saying every expense needs an invoice, Greg replied-all with, "Do you even know what you're doing?"

"What a dirtball," Elliot says. He's breathless like he's already started some serious curls. "You have to have invoices. I bet he's overextended."

"He just bought a new sports car. Like a GT or something," I say.

"That does not sound good." He whispers his rep counts.

"Damn it. What should I do?" I had wanted Elliot to say embezzlement was rare and required deep criminal knowledge. Greg seems generally sleazy, not a mastermind. Instead, Elliot says, "Quit." But then he pauses his rep count. "You don't sign the checks, right?"

"I do sign the checks! I do everything—bookkeeping, HR, web design, anything they can't afford to hire someone for. It's a startup."

Elliot lets out a huge breath like he has moved on to bench presses. "Sounds like his partner is clueless, too," he says. I hear the high ring of metal hitting metal as he releases a weight.

Here's where I pull back. "Joe's a good guy," I say. "He was vocal about me getting a good salary." There's a line here.

"You can't spend it in jail," he says.

"Are you quoting a movie?"

Elliot spouts dialogue from old crime movies whenever he doesn't know what to say. He started it, like, ten years ago, after he had his first daughter and grew anxious under the weight of parenting. It seems a little OCD. But he's pretty good. Some of the actors he mimics are obvious, like Humphrey Bogart or Peter Lorre. Others are obscure, your Ralph Meeker, your Clifton Webb.

"I should go," I say.

At the store, Andrew nicks his finger with the box cutter opening a case of dog treats and acts like it's the end of the world. "Goddamn, why package this like a nuclear bomb?"

On Fridays, we match his product to my invoices and have lunch at a basement pizza place next door. He curses so often and so creatively, I'm only minorly surprised he yells "motherfucker" and sucks his finger before I even get my coat off.

Andrew has angular features and is sometimes goofy, which I like. But our work flirtation is likely fueled by boredom. He complains about his girlfriend, but he's obviously into whatever they have going.

"You're early?" He wipes his forehead with his sleeve.

"Joe asked me to bring over bonuses," I say.

"So we should hop a plane to Mexico?" He hands me a box cutter.

"Or drive to Canada." I carefully cut the plastic on a pallet of Wilderness kibble.

"I'm sure Canada has a stronger extradition policy." He stands, straightens his T-shirt. "I'm just fucking kidding. Why are you looking at me like that?"

I come clean even though it's stressful to tell him we both might be out of a job soon. I ease into it.

"Greg made me write another check yesterday. Fifteen thousand. No invoice. He's taken out a hundred grand in a month."

Andrew leans against the shelves and lets his shoulders sink. With the build-out of this new store, we both thought Greg might straighten up. "Damn it!" says Andrew.

It's really disappointing. We were in on the ground level of a massive pet-store chain. Wholistic pet supplies were sure to take off in Atlanta, Denver, Seattle, San Francisco. We would have this work family and a recognizable brand in every town, so your Pekingese could enjoy a life free from skin conditions and matted fur. Your Puli and Dandie Dinmont Terrier could have an all-natural diet, as they would in the wild. We were going to make the world more goddamn delightful, one light-up toy at a time.

"He's a fucking douche, man. He probably came out of the womb a douche and his mom was like 'Damn it, why is my child such a douche?'" Andrew bends down and yanks boxes from the case. He throws them onto the shelf. "I would never run a business like this."

"Joe's probably liquidating part of his retirement to cover this place, even as we speak." I return to unwinding the plastic from the pallet. When Andrew doesn't answer my trash talk with more trash talk, I look up to see his face frozen in a scowl.

I stand up. "What?"

There's a light touch on my arm, and I hear a voice. "Did you bring the bonuses?"

"Hey, Joe," I say. "Didn't see you there."

"I'd like to pass them out here first." His smile is faint, and I can't tell if he heard me. He's making eye contact, but his brow is cinched with a train track of worry. I'm an asshole.

TELL HIM, Andrew mouths the words.

I lift my purse and pull out the envelope of checks. I hand it over. "Everybody appreciates this," I say. "Your sacrifice."

Andrew rolls his eyes, but I keep my mouth shut.

My brother struggles with sleep and admits that in the wee hours he binges on *Cops*, *CSI*, and, of course, old detective movies. When the fatigue accumulates, he takes a hardcore sleep aid and, around two or so, sleepwalks to the kitchen and eats a leftover casserole or pizza or a whole Tupperware of cookies until my sister-in-law finds him and ushers him back to their room. So, it isn't surprising at midnight when I get the text: *What are you doing about your crooked boss?*

Elliot knows how to project a big-brother/cop-type tone when it suits him. I always went to him for advice in high school: passing classes, getting some guy's attention. But we aren't that kind of family anymore. I don't need an open chain of texts to make me feel obligated.

To be honest, the irony of him becoming a cop this last year sticks in my craw. He acts as though prosecuting criminals has always been his calling. But the first time all our family secrets came out, he took my dad's side.

On the way to church, I shared details it took me months to confess. Elliot looks perfectly glassy eyed, like he will be sick over the steering wheel. He slowly sinks the gas pedal, pushing us to ninety. He ignores the occasional hum of the rumble strip as the tires stray.

I want my brother to concede what he's seen. But it comes out aggressive. "I hope you don't mind the whole church knowing," I tell him.

"What are you talking about?" he says.

"I'm going to report him."

"That's a felony." He looks horrified. "It means serious prison time."

When I don't answer, Elliot knows I'm serious. He yanks the steering wheel toward the service road and floors it through a speed zone. He cuts, tires screeching, into a Ruby Tuesday. His speed launches him over a curb, and he drives through some bushes before hitting a parking barrier. He has a death-grip on the steering wheel. He begins to cough. He opens the door. He throws up on the asphalt.

Two men in jeans and flannels hurry over to check out the situation. From their raised eyebrows, they clearly believe Elliot is drunk. It is on the tip of my tongue to spill our story, to tell them the whole situation. Instead, I stare straight ahead. My brother says he's fine and they take him at his word. One guy hands him a wad of napkins from his to-go bag before walking on. "Take it easy," he says over his shoulder.

Elliot wipes his face.

"If you tell the police, you're no longer my sister," he says.

So perhaps Joe and I will report Greg to the police together. That sounds likely.

I blow smoke through the barred window of our office, a unit in a refurbished cold-storage building stuffed with boxes of pet-food samples and three oversized metal desks. Mine is at the front, and this morning I probably sat for ten minutes rehearsing my opening: *Hey, Joe, I think your partner is stealing. Hey, Joe, your high-school buddy is a thief. Hey, Joe, your friend of twenty years is actively ruining your life.* I hear footfalls in the stairwell and chuck the cigarette through the bars. I have to run to unlock the door.

"Sorry I'm late," says Joe. He shakes the rain from his baseball cap over the rubber mat. Usually, he brings a box of cinnamon rolls and a caddy of coffee to our monthly meetings, but today he's empty-handed, and his eyes are red.

I slide into my seat, holding the reports. "You OK?" I ask.

He sinks into the office chair and rubs his forehead. He takes the reports like he needs something to hold, like he doesn't know what to do with his hands. "I'm going to be honest," he says. "We can't make payroll."

"There's money in the account," I say. This is the time to tell him.

"I wrote a check for the build-out before looking at the account," he says. It's clear he's bewildered. He shakes his head. "I guess we just needed way more product than I anticipated."

He really has no idea. How is that possible? I can barely resist the urge to shout: GREG WITHDREW YOUR MONEY. HE MADE CHECKS OUT TO HIMSELF. HE DOESN'T CARE ABOUT YOU.

"Don't worry. I'm going to meet with Greg and see about getting a line of credit. Otherwise, I'm going to liquidate some of my own funds," he says.

"Don't."

He smiles a little. "Payroll can't be late. But I might have to let some floor staff go."

This feels like a punch to the gut. "Joe, listen."

Repeating violence—a fire, a murder, a rape—holds a moment of release. But if the story isn't offered, it can feel like a thick worm pulled from your throat, like the segmented body writhing over your tongue. For a long time, I hadn't talked about it.

When Elliot asks the women's Bible-study leader to invite me to a prayer breakfast, I am livid. "I have a therapist," I say. She's an empathetic listener, free through the school, unconnected to our family.

I decide not to tell this tight-lipped deaconess anything. But there she is when I arrive at church with Elliot and Dad. She touches my forearm. She knows something, but I feel certain Elliot has left Dad out of it. Some shadowy figure, a troubled neighbor kid, an older teen babysitter, has become the abstract person to pin it on.

The deaconess' whisper is minty. "Jesus' love has no limits." She offers to buy me coffee and "study the word sometime" before I head to college.

She leads me to a seat with her amazingly tight grip. Her Bible-study group fills the first row. I squeeze in beside another teen, a girl who reeks of cigarettes and who will eventually trace the crosshatched scars on my forearm during the opening prayer.

And the altar call. The altar call. People raise their hands in surrender to a sermon on forgiveness or repentance or peace or something. The pastor clutches a microphone, eyes closed, and testifies with palm upraised. "Surely, God's grace is here," he says. And the bass comes in with the first few notes of "At the Cross." It sucks the air from the room and makes the hairs on my arms and legs stand up.

This Sunday, it seems all for Elliot. He slowly walks to the altar. And he cries, and people cry with him, and other men, some our age, grasp his shoulder and hang on. Elliot lifts his folded prayer-hands to his face for two hymns, though altar calls usually last only one.

What could he want God to do about this?

Elliot stands and turns so I finally see his whole face and it is blank, like a huge burden is gone, like he can float out of the building and right down the street and into the rest of his life. He's given it to

Christ, of course, and everyone around him cries with joy. He doesn't even have to say who needs atonement in our family.

I stare at the altar and think, Well, that's convenient.

One morning before work, I open an email from the accountant asking for the quarterlies. The answer to stopping Greg's embezzlement becomes obvious.

I get up and go to CVS for a thumb drive. I feel like a sleepwalker going through rote actions, my intuition as a guide. I will cut out early so Greg won't have the chance to fire me. I can't bear that. At the office, I photocopy bank statements, cancelled checks, stock certificates, and reconciliations on the ancient copier and shove a set in my purse. I call a courier to pick up the other set. Then I email a full explanation of Greg's theft to the accountant, who is legally required to do something. For good measure, I copy the head of the firm, whose name I have to pull from their website.

Someone will call Greg or Joe and broach the subject of embezzlement. I watch YouTube videos of cats and wait. I don't know why. Maybe I hope Joe will hear first and call. Of course, I couldn't tell him the whole story, not to his face. At 2 p.m., I pack my stuff, put on my coat, and turn off the lights.

As I shoulder my purse, I hear the teeth of keys in the lock. Light from the soda machine spills in from the hallway.

"Where you going?" says Greg. He looks mildly surprised.

"I'm heading out," I say.

He blocks the door, his body outlined in blue from the soda machine. I grip two keys between my fingers. Why am I afraid? He's never been physically aggressive. I just imagine if he is willing to screw over his friend, he might be a sociopath.

"It's not even three o'clock. But, OK. You're knocking off early," says Greg.

"Andrew needs me to stock at the South Loop store." I hope this will move him, but he just stands there.

"Listen, Carrie. You've been in over your head for a while. We're letting you go," he says. There's that smirk from the staff party.

I'm shaking, but I still say, "Fuck you." I hope this will get him to move, but he doesn't. His face is smooth and shiny with sweat. His mouth is open. He smells like the whiskeys he likely downed at a business lunch.

"Better hope nothing's missing in this office," he says.

"Can you move?" My pitch is so high it surprises me.

He jumps out of the way as if he hasn't even thought about the dynamic until now. He has the nerve to look offended.

Outside, the cool air hits me, and I pause on the sidewalk. In Greg's reserved parking spot is his GT, all chrome and bright yellow. Keys between my fingers, I consider running them the length of the car, the yellow paint curling like a ribbon. But I just stand there.

Above me, the office is lit a murky white against the overcast autumn afternoon. He has probably come to throw away check copies or change the books. But I already have confirmation the courier made the delivery. I imagine Greg ripping open drawers and binders, trying to locate the statements.

Eventually, it grows depressing to stand there and watch a window, and I head home.

Even before that uncomfortable day at church, I'd decided to do it.

I have an airtight plan—pack a bag, say I'm sleeping at a friend's, park a few blocks away, walk up the street wearing my dark navy jacket.

Dad will be watching baseball in the downstairs family room. He will have dozed by the sixth inning.

I could burn down our house so his skin crackles and leaps and whistles as it catches. My brother isn't home. Who would suspect me? But TV taught me there is always a trail of microbes and receipts and neighbors without blinds who stand in front of their windows at night.

Our house is built into the Allegheny foothills, an ugly split-level with two bedroom windows like eyeholes in a mask. I pull the spray paint from my bag even before I get up the drive. I think of the adolescent girls in our neighborhood; a couple are just now ten. Dad rarely goes outside, but he could ask them to cut his lawn or walk our dog or some other bullshit. He could give one of them a gift. He gave me a bike.

The door of our two-car garage is bright white in the flood lamp.

I stretch on the balls of my feet and follow the paint line to crouch on the cement, keeping the letters even and tall, so everyone will see it after passing through the subdivision entrance. I stand back to survey the squashed letters with slight unease: RAPIST.

☾

I knock on the door at the rear entrance of the new store, knowing Andrew will be counting receipts. Even through the tinted safety glass, his face appears bloodless, and he holds up a finger before releasing the locks. He has one hand shoved in his hoodie pocket. I see the box cutter bulging from the other pocket, which seems over-the-top. "I was afraid you were Greg. They haven't changed the lock on this back door," he says.

I hand him a bag. "Joe wanted me to bring over this new security camera so the guy can install it tomorrow. Are you done? Want a drink?"

"Sure," he says. He returns to a stack of receipts, pivoting so stiffly I wonder what news he has to tell me. "Do you mind if I smoke?" he says.

"Of course not."

He lights a cigarette, and I slide onto the edge of the desk. He gathers the bank bag and the rubber bands he's using to bind rolls of quarters. He says, "Man, when Joe changed that first lock, I thought it was over."

"Yeah. He was in the office on the phone with his lawyers."

Cigarette clinging to his lips, Andrew makes a hammock of his sweatshirt and loads in rolls of change. "Then Greg comes around 8 a.m. Wants to talk to me."

I shove my hands in my pockets. "It's not like you're going to unlock the doors for him."

"No way," says Andrew. He kneels beside the safe.

I imagine Greg standing at the glass doors in the middle of the South Loop, face inches from the glass, his shoulders tense as he starts yelling to open the door. Unsurprising.

Andrew stuffs the rolls of change into the tiny safe. "He said you were lying. You didn't know what you were doing. You lost the paperwork. All that bullshit. Right through the motherfucking door."

"Wow," I say.

Andrew returns to the desk to stuff the cash into a bank bag, a few stacks of tens and twenties. He pulls a single twenty from a stack. "Petty cash. For drinks," he says. He actually shakes the bill at me. I suddenly feel nauseated.

Andrew returns to the safe and shoves the bag inside. "Like I'd buy that crap about you. You're straight as an arrow." He crushes his cigarette on the table. "Seriously. Thanks for saving our asses, though."

"No problem," I say.

He slides into his coat and pulls the keys from his pocket. "I'm so glad we don't have to listen to that douche's same five stories anymore. He was the worst."

"Yeah. The worst."

In some ways, Elliot has always been tough. At least, he's always been comfortable in his own body. And he's always been fast.

The foothills of the Allegheny are slick and nearly impossible to run in the winter. But Elliot leans so far forward in his sprint, he appears perpendicular to the asphalt, as if with a little effort he can fly over the street, grazing it lightly with his fingertips.

Though my lungs burn with frozen air, I haven't fallen behind, not even a yard. On our last leg home he'll shout "you got this" as we race to the garage. But he always reaches it first, smacking the wood hard enough to rattle the chains of the automatic door.

He has been bugging me to revive our morning runs for weeks. When he saw me sneak from the bathroom, crossing my arms over my chest to hide the red hatches, he said "tomorrow morning."

Anyway, the sound of Dad's early activities—the whistling and the tinkling of silverware against a cereal bowl—have awakened in me a desire to shiv him at the breakfast table. The tension has only risen as each morning Dad absently taps his coffee mug with his spoon long after the milk has dissolved. I agree to a run.

Elliot and I run the side streets, which go the whole winter unplowed. Our route drops onto a service road, which we pound to the highway. We always get coffee and a sandwich with egg and country ham at a place for truckers. We will eat outside and sit on the picnic tables beneath the truck-stop sign.

At this moment, we can still say anything. And this is the point where I hope he'll share my grief. Witness it. In a few months, I'll have a therapist and it will all come out. Right now, all I have to say is: I want out of my own skin.

I need to—
put my hand in a car door
slam a hot iron to my face

jump off an overpass
peel the skin down to the white fat with a fillet knife
soak in bleach
stick my fingers in a food processor
drink a mug of antifreeze
I need, for just a few minutes, to not be in this body. This body, it seems, is the source of my trouble.

Our steps wind down as we reach the picnic tables at the far end of the parking lot, where we pant for breath. "I need to see a counselor," I say.

Elliot has been going on and on about his girlfriend, who will eventually become my sister-in-law.

"Elliot," I say. "Dad molested me." I slowly explain the when and the how, but I'm waiting for affirmation. Did I think of yelling for him? Yes. But I was nine, ten, and eleven, and Dad whispered so many threats. His large body became a mass of hair and sweat and endless flesh. I clawed at the sheets. Yes. But I never seemed able to fill my lungs enough to scream.

"You didn't hear a thing?" I say. "You didn't hear a door creak? Nothing?"

"No," he says. "No." He slowly shakes his head. It looks like he won't stop this ridiculous action.

I sit on the wet picnic table. Elliot's face drains. He tries to sit beside me but misses the slick edge and falls. He stands but slips on the gravel again and catches himself with one hand, looking like a sad acrobat. "So bad," he says. "So bad."

A woman getting donuts with her boyfriend walks over and asks if I'm OK. She clearly imagines my brother is an abusive boyfriend. I tell her it's fine. Though she's uncertain, she walks to her car.

Elliot gives up on sitting and paces for minutes, tennis shoes crunching the gravel, his arms anchored to the back of his head like he's stretching. He will talk to our dad. Yes. He will talk to Dad.

I can see by his expression his resolve is already slipping, though, even as he says what he'll do. So I hold him to put him at ease.

Maggie Graber

Why I Shouldn't Be
an FBI Special Agent

Friends, today on this rainy April afternoon,
while searching the job boards of the Internet,
cup of coffee near my hands hovering
above the alphabet, in my new Southwestern leggings
and Chicago Blackhawks hoodie, I learned
I could apply to be a special agent for the FBI.
And before you think I'm fucking with you
I fit all of the requirements. Bachelor's degree.
Driver's license. Right age range. I'm a
U.S. citizen that's been working for at least 36 months.
It's all there. And they even try to sell it too.
Say how every day's different. An ongoing investigation
in the morning. Testify at court before lunch. As if
I'm going to apply to the FBI purely for the wide net
of pace-changing experiences, as if they know
everyone is distracted these days,
that we need constant stimulation or else we dissolve
into a pool of red salt. And I'd be lying if I said
I'm not considering it. I'm a poet, after all.
What if there's an X-Files-type gig lurking in the future
and I never get to write all those extraterrestrial poems
inside me because I felt pressured to "stay in my field."
These are questions worth considering.
I'd probably be required to carry a gun,
and I'd probably be expected to use it, which

I do not want. The only time I've ever fired a gun
was in a cornfield in southern Illinois near the confluence
of the Ohio and Mississippi on the first of November
a few years back. An accordion player
with dreadlocks and a Robert E. Lee tattoo on his stomach
was in town for a show. A friend of the girl
I was into at the time, we all went to get bagels after beers
from Winston, the old man with the bagel cart
who loved shoveling carbohydrates to drunken college students.
We talked about the guns in his trunk, and because
I was curious, and because it felt like an experience
I needed to have, and because I thought
it could maybe impress her, before we knew it,
we were in the next town over, the cold metal heavy
in my hand, and me aiming the barrel
into the quiet nothingness of that field.
I fired twice. Once straight ahead, the second cocked
a little higher. The next morning, I woke up, panicked
that the bullet strayed through a window,
found a home in an old woman who couldn't sleep,
who was reading the paper and drinking tea
at her kitchen table. Or that it greeted an older man
getting out of his pickup truck. Or that it found a dog.
The next few days I kept checking the local news
for stories about mysterious gun deaths, and thanked
whatever higher power I needed to every time I found nothing.
Which only means nothing got reported.
Which is to say, in another universe, the bullets
never landed, that they're still flying, defying
the laws of physics and gravity on a trajectory around
the planet, making small Saturns of the Earth.
Those bullets that sped away like two drag racers,
like fireworks exploding in my hands
with the small balls of cotton in my ears,
the way this girl always made me want
to try new things even though she stayed behind
the driving wheel the entire time
and the next week I got my first tattoo

of the symbol for Pi on my left wrist.
Which is to say circles. Which is to say diameters.
Which is to say the bullets never landed,
that I can't scrounge the dirt for the heaviness of lead
to weigh down my palms. Gravity doesn't apply
to the imagination. If I'm hollow on the inside,
just two bullets in a lake of air, it's because
I believed a gun could give me love. It's because
I grew up white in middle-class America with the idea
of violence, but not violence. Which is to say
the mind can justify anything. Even this poem.

Jonathan Winston Jones

Willa Cather's Ghost

I. Willa Cather's Ghost

Permit me to let objects and entities carry this roving narrative, which I liken to a cracked mirror. Permit me to let this mirror judder upon the faded plaster but never shatter so as to offer a fragmented yet true reflection of a rattled world of shadows and light.

My feet rest on the rich, red rug my preacher husband bought from Afghanistan. I hope it did not enrich the Taliban. One of our two Siamese cats, brothers and life partners, already puked on it, and I cleaned it with my sock first thing this morning. Too tired I was from my cumbersome autoimmune disease, this well-played insult to my body by my eccentric white blood cells, to fathom a proper cleaning.

I remember the Taliban. The word "Taliban" sounded to me like talisman when I heard my high school social studies teacher, the brawny Speedo-wearing swim team coach, utter the name in 2000. That afternoon on a sneezy spring day in the Nebraska railroad town of my childhood, the word "Taliban" on the brawny coach's lips sounded prophetic, like it was always meant to happen. Then, a year or so later, the crashing airplanes chopped down the Towers. The morning when the Towers fell, I was smoking in the garden in the courtyard of the 1920s Georgian dorm at college, which used to be a hospital during the Depression for patients rounded up during an outbreak of polio in Lincoln, Nebraska.

Lincoln, Nebraska, in Dust Bowl days of the Depression, was like a loose society woman, according to the writer Mari Sandoz in her novel *Capital City*. Lincoln, Nebraska, in Mari Sandoz's view, would put out for any businessman, any guy with rolls of crash cash, or just credit. Not even necessarily the best credit. He could end up broke on bad futures, speculation, trying to corner the grain market without success.

Trying to put Ceres, Demeter, the goddess of grain and fertility, in a corner equals failure. She'll rise up against you. She'll conspire to flood your low-lying coastal entrepôts. She'll even work behind the scenes to turn your country over to a bedlam of Russian internet trolls who masquerade via social media as conservative commentators and dupe the populace into anointing a compromised and crooked sleaze king from Queens to be the president. All to remind you who runs the show.

In the college dorm courtyard, I befriended a young lady because I craved a cigarette. With her spikey, red hair and fuzzy armpits reminiscent of city-states of fire ants, she seemed to me a total smoker. Turns out she didn't smoke. But she claimed to see Willa Cather's writerly ghost. The ghost of Willa Cather, she alleged, hovered in her dorm room closet. I investigated. There I found a large bag of Idaho potatoes sprouting like Chia pets while in the background the Towers smoldered on the television. When the Towers fell into trembling heaps of ash and fire, she told me to put my swishy homo-man hips to work and microwave her up some dinner. As she feasted, she sang of Second Comings, of sperm and Armageddon, of old stories burning to be told again and again.

II. *The House of Radical Lesbian Feminist Angels*

Our gray Siamese cat's bumblebee, a little stuffed animal holding a red heart that reads "Bee Mine." It belonged to Mary's dead dog Smokey. The dog is buried with Mary and her wife, Joanne, in a country cemetery outside of Little Cedar, Iowa.

Mary's mother, Florence, now almost 100, is still alive last I heard. Florence, the widow of a dairy farmer, wrote Mary's surviving wife, Joanne, before Joanne herself died at 59, saying, "It's so sad you young girls are gone so soon, and here am I still alive, God knows why, not certain if there's room left in heaven or hell for me."

Florence was born in Little Cedar. It is her family plot going back to the 1870s where Mary and Joanne are buried. Mary's mother in her young years had sandy brown hair and a pretty face but not too pretty, the kind of tough, solid woman you would expect to be a dairy farmer's wife. She married a rugged blond soldier back from the war ten years her senior named Sandy. Mary and her lesbian friends would joke about her parents, Florence and Sandy, having perfect names for an old lesbian couple of the Greatest Generation.

In her bottlecap glasses, Mary played the accordion at her parties, even when she was sick, with her dog Smokey, a fluffy Schipperke, nipping at the heels of her guests. Smokey, a beat-up stray, followed Mary home to her Victorian worker's cottage from the hawkish and phallic marble war monument in Chicago's Logan Square neighborhood when Mary was four years into cancer, four years into chemo, four years into puking. Smokey was particularly fond of biting the heels of Mary's Chinese friend and comrade, T.T., who lived across the street. The old neighborhood, those two houses across from each other, one a blue worker's cottage, one a brownstone, where T.T. and Mary each lived for decades and saw their collective love of left-wing revolution fade. In the early seventies, they revered the socialist paradigm, their idealism strong. But they grew disappointed, disillusioned like almost everyone.

Mary, for her part, probably never got on board with capitalism. Instead, she tended bees. Bees, she said, are gentle. Bees won't sting you unless you have it coming. A swarm of bees got loose in her car when she and wife Joanne were driving the swarm back to Logan Square from the Chicago suburbs. She and Joanne covered themselves in bedsheets. They pulled up to a friend's house on the way back to the city to try to corral the swarm. Their friend said they looked like children dressing up as ghosts on Halloween, like Mary might have done on the farm outside of Little Cedar when she was a husky girl with a plain face with sheets for a costume. "Boo!" she'd say in her low, dead-pan voice, to the amusement of her mother Florence.

Mary's nephew, a mixed-race African -American fellow around my age, early to mid-thirties, inherited her irreverent sense of humor. After Joanne's memorial service in Iowa, we were eating roast beef and buns in the fellowship hall of the Methodist church. As Mary's mother Florence stood, cane in hand, talking about the fantastically dedicated lesbian and gay friends who cared for Mary and Joanne when they were dying, Mary's nephew chuckled and pointed to the block letters on the back of the folding chairs. "Meth Church, they all say," he whispered.

Mary left a big box of keepsakes tucked away in an upstairs closet behind a bunch of antique chairs and a bed frame. Joanne, grief-stricken after Mary's death, probably did not ever realize it was there.

At the last moment, we found it. We could not pitch it. We moved it to the basement of our new place, which my preacher husband and I bought to start over. In the box, Mary's baby book. A story Mary wrote when she was eight about the Confederation of the Iroquois. Love letters from the woman Mary dated while she was renovating the blue worker's cottage, which Mary left to wife Joanne, which Joanne left to my preacher husband when she died, which we called "The House of Radical Lesbian Feminist Angels," where we lived for exactly 1,014 days. There we painted the interior walls shades of cheerful beige called champagne and flan. There we ate pies every summer made from cherries of the tree Mary planted in the back yard. There we accented the gingerbread of the eaves with a blushing hue of red. Leave it to the gays to tart up the Victorian worker's cottage formerly inhabited by lesbians.

There I wept the day we sold and left. I saw Mary in her late thirties, her short hair graying, drinking coffee in Chinese comrade T.T.'s brownstone, in the upstairs flat she rented from him, and reading in the newspaper ads that the Victorian worker's cottage across the street was for sale. I saw Mary on the roof, armed with her tool belt, putting down tar paper. I saw Mary in the kitchen, the plaster stripped down to the lathing, wearing a denim top and a flowery skirt, an unusual getup for her, self-proclaimed butch dyke that she was. Before I turned over my keys to the new owners, I wept in every room, even in the basement as I watched the 1-800-JUNK guys clean out all the broken antiques the lesbians stockpiled.

It's hard to know why these things happen. Why right out of college in Nebraska did I get a Fulbright to England, like Sylvia Plath I secretly fancied, and while there feel like Sylvia Plath, without the courage to turn on the gas, but with my eccentric white blood cells getting the message, getting down to business to trash the place? After getting so ill so young, why did I change my plans, forgoing the more ambitious life I had in mind and happening upon the path to Chicago to meet the preacher?

How did these two women buried with their dead dog Smokey in a sparse, country cemetery in Iowa become such a part of me? Why do I ring the prayer bell for them, before all others who have died, every evening?

III. Jail Time

I suspect the answer to these questions comes down to jail time, jail time best prefaced with rambling syntax and rhyme. En route to the answer, I'll mash together debris from long ago, like the failed plotting of a sixteenth-century Italian banker to restore Catholicism to Elizabethan England, with today's political intrigues, namely the retweet from the sleazy, kingly presidential brat of an unverified video showing the Virgin Mary allegedly being defaced by Muslims. The original tweet came from an anti-Muslim group in Britain, Elizabeth I's great isle of the Reformation, the tolerant dominion that gave birth to the constitutional democracy of the United States.

Elizabeth, the Renaissance princess who did time in the Tower of London and loathed religious persecution, chose to embody the Virgin when she became the sovereign to usurp the goddess iconography in the hearts of subjects who missed the ancient Catholic religion. Elizabeth, the heretical spinster queen of Europe's boondocks, sent munitions and a lavish clockwork organ to the Ottoman Sultan to enlist Muslims to help her fight the Bible-thumbing kings on the Continent who wanted to see her dead and her country conquered. And Elizabeth, haunted by the execution of her mother by her bully of a father, Henry VIII, did not want a monster husband or his monster son. Both would create temptation to take her down, whether they authored the deed or were persuaded. She called babies "winding sheets," meaning death shrouds. Such are the fates of women who must wear the fanged ermine robes of kings.

A king is a loaded thing. Full of macho insecurity. A king needs to be petted. A king needs an audience imprisoned.

My mother is presently imprisoned in Wahoo, Nebraska, for methamphetamines. Wahoo, Nebraska, has the distinction of being the birthplace of first-wave feminist and writer Tillie Olsen, who must have been one lonely Jew as a child there in the early 1900s. I have telephoned the prison in Wahoo several times to get details: visitation rules, how to send my mother a letter, the digits of her inmate number, 9409.

My mother, by way of backstory, was sweetly sixteen when she became a mother. She got hooked on meth during my bruised adolescence while working nonstop, while trying to be both father and mother, the lonely leader of our ramshackle, debt-ridden household.

I suspect meth gave her energy. I suspect for a time it made her feel like she could manage, thrive. But out of the shadows meth came to steal our meager bliss and, like a pack of greedy, diseased wolves, gnaw at our flesh, with the stress of her addiction and incarcerations contributing, I believe, to the eccentricity of my white blood cells which trash my body, which compel me to humbly take my place among the many walking wounded of a long "drug war" on people of color, on the poor. In the House of Radical Lesbian Feminist Angels, I wept for three grave days when my mother last disappeared and was found behind bars.

Recently, I got it in my head to visit my mother in prison but didn't think she'd be happy to see her high-strung, overachiever son. Instead, I wrote her a note describing the objects outside the window of my office: the dark, solemn windows of the gothic Tribune Tower across the smelly Chicago River, the high-rise hookup Hyatt where boobs and butts sometimes stare out at me at midday, the pinking sky of dusk glowing over the many twinkling lights of the skyscrapers where others work into the evening, though I suspect none of the other office workers at this altitude have mothers incarcerated for methamphetamines in Wahoo, Nebraska. I doubt many of them have a mother with inmate number 9409.

IV. My Committee

So, does anyone on my committee of writerly ghosts have any ideas on how to reconstruct this broken story?

Plath, could you take your head out of the oven for a minute? I need you to help me figure out the mood for when I was in England stuck in that byzantine infirmary at age 22, very ill and very alone, and an old guy in the bed next to me named Roger, probably with dementia, bless his heart, got up in the middle of the night and started peeing. For an old guy, the stream of his pee was quite forceful, the arc like water passing out of the nozzle of a hose with one's thumb pressed to it, and I woke up to find my bedsheets becoming rather wet.

Our Cather, who art dressed in drag in heaven, how about a hand with lyricism? Readers of my work whose spirits feel female or gender fluid always seem to get it, but the manly types often do not. Remember how Ernest Hemingway always criticized your work as being clichéd? What a spoiled baby from a tony Chicago suburb he was, whereas you hoofed it like man through the isolated and woolly Nebraska grasslands. Let's not include him on this committee. No matter how long it takes, once we have accomplished something with this writing, once this work is known, let's rub it in.

O Whitman! My conversation partner across time, are you over last night's intemperate wine hangover from that bar in the French Quarter where a beefcake daddy goosed you? Let's talk about the freedom and responsibility of the artist in America right now, the hard-won freedom of the artist to go where she'd like, however she'd like, to become her own master, his own mistress, their own creation, their own "good-fortune." Let's discuss the responsibility of the artist to love and nourish, perhaps even rescue the fenceless, open-handed soul of our nation struggling so hard to be born anew. When I recite your verse to myself while splashing in the bathtub, I hear the angels. I know this may sound rather sentimental for the likes of you, but is it possible, Mr. Whitman, that poems and stories when written in love can become, say, the song of hope for us from those we have lost or those we love who lost their way, whom we may never see on Earth again, whose words we hear forever whenever we pick up the pen?

And, last but not least, on the matter of the power of the word to bring forth light or smear darkness through the hearts of humans, on the matter of the light that the word has the power to draw from within, the light that to darkness can never give in, writer or writers of John's Gospel, what advice have you on how to begin?

Brianna McNish

Little Houses

The last tag sale before the end of the world only sold vinyl records. Old porcelain dolls with chipped, hollow skulls. Watery lemonade, made courtesy of the seller's five-year-old daughter, that went warm under the blistering, late-August sun.

"That's it?" asked Alanie after spending nearly an hour rifling through an old box filmed with dust. Inside, there were only cracked Motown records that surely must have belonged to the seller's grandmother. The boy who was trying to sell them to her could not have been older than seventeen or eighteen, and her complaints were met with the boy's agitated apology and perfunctory, "Look, my mom will be home in fifteen minutes."

Fifteen minutes dragged into thirty and this mysterious mother never showed. Alanie began to doubt if there ever was a mother; parents who left their children behind to endure whatever hardships the end of the world promised were becoming increasingly common, according to the news. They were dumping babies on doorsteps. They were abandoning them in grocery-store aisles. They were left at school. From the principal's office, they waited for someone to pick up the house phone, but their calls were met with static and a disabled landline.

"Is she dead?" mouthed Alanie thoughtlessly. She fit her finger into the gaping hole inside a doll's skull, hoping, maybe, if she dug far enough, if she smiled hard enough, perhaps she could distract herself from the stupidity of her question.

"This is my grandmother's stuff," the boy said. "She died and so now we have to sell it."

"No, I meant—."

"My mom will be back in fifteen minutes," returned the boy flatly.

A five-year-old girl—likely the boy's sister—swiped her brown Barbie doll through the stuffy heat as if she were trying to swat away a fly. Alanie watched the five-year-old with a flicker of envy. How wasteful it was to let such a perfectly fine, healthy child play in such blistering heat, to let her become exposed to the maggots, the rashes, the fevers, the *everything*. Alanie wished she could be afforded the same carelessness. She wished her baby, or whatever was left of it, had stayed buried within her instead of leaving so soon. She liked the idea of becoming a walking funeral, a portable casket. Instead, her body emptied itself and expunged all life within her in a heartbeat. Nothing resided within her and made a home there. Alanie was empty now. There was no baby. Only her.

"I'm only here for the weekend," she continued. "This is a great place to see the world end. On this website, they listed this place in the Top-Ten Best Places to Watch the End of Times." When the boy seemed reluctant to ask where their town ranked, she quipped, "This place ranked number seven."

"Did you want to buy the doll or not, lady?"

She hadn't realized she was still fingering its empty porcelain skull.

"Sure," she said. "I'll take it."

The doll was three dollars. Overpriced, thought Alanie, considering it had been broken, considering the clothes that had been fitted over its solid shape hardly fit. But she still bought her, because a part of her believed this was what her baby would have looked like: small, pocket-sized, dark-haired.

"Are you going to watch the meteor crash to earth?" Alanie asked. She was genuinely concerned for this boy and his sister, who had been waiting more than fifteen minutes for their mother. She was concerned for the girl trapped in a fantasy with her long-haired Barbie doll. "There's a lot of amazing watch parties all over. There's one in the town center, right by the—."

"I don't do parties," said the boy stiffly. He frowned a little. "Plus, why the hell would I want to see the world blow up with other people when I can just stream it on my phone or something?"

"I'm sorry," she said.

"It's fine. But we don't have much time left."

"I know."

"And my mom is supposed to come back in fifteen minutes."

"I know."

"And I was supposed to meet Jack to play *Halo*, but, obviously, that shit isn't going to happen."

"Yes," she said, even if she hadn't known this, "I know."

He spoke as if this thing, this impossible thing that would lead to the world's end, had been an inconvenience meant to ruin his entire day.

It was only then she noticed he had been squirming a little. He was becoming a floundering fish before her eyes. He was trying to escape from himself. Alanie recognized the feeling because she had laid in bed alone trying to do the same for weeks. It never staved away the blistering heat. The meteors would continue to draw nearer; fertility rates would continue to plummet; the mortality rates would skyrocket; the neglected children would remain abandoned without anyone to fully explain what was happening. It was hot, unbearably hot.

When she looked up, she saw the house for what felt like the first time: It was consumed by vines stretched like splayed hands over its yellow facade. The windows were shattered. There was no front door or a mesh frame to enclose it. There were pots filled with un-watered weeds.

The five-year-old kept playing with her dolls.

Alanie realized she had her entire hand in the head of a doll with a cracked-open skull.

"That one's five dollars."

"Perfect," she said. Alanie reached for her pocket again but found only a crumpled twenty and several quarters. She emptied the money from her wallet and pressed it into his expectant palm. When else would she ever need money again?

The boy blinked, momentarily stunned.

"Keep the change," she said. "Please."

The boy pocketed the money. She held the two broken baby dolls to her chest.

Meanwhile, Alanie stared past the boy at the house where their family lived, where they once ate with their mother and pretended to feel like everything was whole. She wondered how long it would take for the world to finally break all those little houses apart.

Sarah Freligh

Rummage

You will remember how strangers arrived empty handed and carried away folding chairs and board games and rugs rolled and fastened with rope; left with beach towels and fleece and the polka-dotted dish that belonged to your dog Pedro, who chased the trash truck every Tuesday; left with plates and cups and plastic spatulas, and the glass bowl that once held candy, the cellophane squares of caramel that your mother's boyfriend promised to give you if you were good.

When you were very good, two, one for each nipple. Three for the zipper.

You will never forget how caramel fills, how it smothers the mouth.

Jonathan Minila

We Even Look Like Family

He arrived on time. It was his mother's house. Nervously, he slid the paper from his pocket and read the name: Cristina Gutiérrez. He said it over in his head, and lower down read, "You call her Cristi." He whispered, "Cristi," and rang the doorbell. He went over everything in his head. Don't worry, they'd told him, on the chance that you forget something, they'll help you. Fortunately, he had a good memory.

The soft sound of the doorbell chimed. The clock started. He heard the steps of someone hurrying down the stairs. His niece and nephew, who had the strange habit of competing to see who could open the door. The first thing you always say is not to open the door to strangers. So that's what he did.

"Don't open the door to strangers," he said to Cati (Catalina) and Edu (Eduardo), who were now fighting to hug him.

"Uncle! Uncle!" they shouted as they pounced. He immediately felt at home. He felt wanted.

He heard the voice of their mother—"Who is it, kids?"—and flashed them a sign to stop them from answering.

"Shhhh ...."

"Santa Claus!" Edu shouted, then laughed.

Edu is your favorite.

"Crazy," he said, and ruffled Edu's hair like he imagined you did for all your favorite nephews.

"Who?" his mother asked as she came down the stairs.

He hid behind a wall, like when you were a kid.

"Cristi!" he exclaimed.

"Alejandro!" screamed his frightened mother. "Are you crazy?" Then she hugged him and kissed him on the nose. The gesture moved him considerably. He felt on the verge of tears.

His mother excitedly ushered him upstairs to greet his brother, Cati's father; his brother's wife Ximena, you call her Xime; and his sister Fernanda, single, thirty-five, accountant. For a moment he felt uncomfortable. He didn't know what to do. His brother seemed to notice. He stood, hugged him, and delivered one of his classic lines.

"Are we really this ugly?" he asked, slapping him on the back. "We even look like family."

Family, family ….

He quickly found his confidence and fiercely returned his brother's hug. This was his brother. You only see him once a year, at Christmas Eve dinner.

He sat down with them, kept up a friendly conversation, like every December 24, with laughter and jokes. His niece and nephew ran from one side of the room to the other, begging him to watch their tricks. The moment's warmth gave him goosebumps. This is what he'd always wanted, and now he had it. A big, lovely family. A delicious dinner. He looked reflexively at his watch.

His mother sidled over to him. They chatted about more serious things and reminisced about his childhood.

"You were uncontrollable," she said as she squeezed his nose. He kissed her hand.

They moved to the table. The children were restless.

"Are we ready to open presents now?" they asked over and over again.

"After dinner, tricksters," their grandmother answered.

He then felt the acute absence of his father. His place was empty. He died while you were away.

They began with a flavorful salad. Your favorite. Then came the duck, accompanied by a golden potato puree, and raspberry cake for dessert. They talked about everything. He felt happy. Even when he argued with his brother and then when they made up. They hugged fiercely. He was a bit drunk by then. They talked about their father and cried a little.

They made their way to the living room and began to pass out gifts. He hadn't brought any. It's not necessary, they'd told him. He was tempted to look at his watch but didn't want to. Enjoy the moment, enjoy the moment, he told himself over and over again.

His niece and nephew played with their gifts. His mother laughed joyously. He tried on the sweater they'd given him. It was a beautiful moment interrupted by the sound of a bell.

Everyone suddenly relaxed. The woman playing the role of his mother stopped laughing and took off her wig. The man and the woman who for a few hours had played his siblings began to remove their makeup. The niece and nephew stopped playing and went into the bedroom where their real parents were waiting for them. A man in a suit entered through a door. It was the agent who had sold him the package.

"Mr. Alejandro." He handed him a paper. "Thank you for purchasing this beautiful moment from us. I truly hope that you've enjoyed your Christmas Eve dinner. We recorded everything if you want the souvenir, although that's sold separately. Would you do me a favor and sign here? Thank you, how kind. Be careful and don't forget that we're available year-round. Call us whenever you feel lonely."

He shook the man's hand and took a last look around the house. He saw the actors putting on their coats. He didn't say good-bye. He exited onto the street and headed off toward his real house, where he knew no one was waiting for him.

—Translated from the Spanish by Will Stockton

Sarah Layden

Jumper

Our small screens replayed the moment when the student leapt from the campus center balcony. We were there but witnessed nothing. We were training our tiny cameras to see the blue sky dotted by a line of towers; the hot-dog-eating contest in the food court; the spaghetti-sauce splatters (again) in the employee break-room microwave; the patients out the window walking slow to the cancer hospital, slow from the cancer hospital, one smoking a cigarette around an oxygen mask. We were spies in plain sight, watching each other online, noticing the ex now watching someone new. We checked our teeth and hair and nostrils in the reflections of our phones. We turned the bathroom into a hall of mirrors, gilt tarnished, a line of selves, stretching in opposite directions, with a single face. One of us was recording a song and caught the jumper in the frame. The video made the local news and logged more views than the politician who was caught doing—what had he done? That was weeks ago, or maybe months. The singer didn't miss a note; days later she signed her first record contract. Now we are watching the jumper video and asking how on Earth we missed it. We were *right there*. Later, we felt as if we'd missed nothing. We'd caught and cradled the moment on our hard drives and caressed the buttons to make the video replay on a loop. We were there. I was. He wasn't my student. It wasn't like I knew him. With each viewing I am drawn to the lock of my own hair, wind-lifted, that appears to wrap the falling man in a hug. I say *man*, but I mean *boy*. I say *hair*, but I mean *noose*. Then the wind dies, the wind drops, the wind does everything it is supposed to do, because it is the wind. This can't be changed. Paused at the right moment, the jumper hovers, eyes open and staring into the lens, without judgment. His being a premonition of stillness. Fixed, immutable. The play button is an arrow pointing to a distance we can't see or know or cross. Our fingers itch with the pushing.

Simon Shieh

in which I go with him

I meet him in a myth about a man's head
and a brick wall.

I meet him through his car window
on an empty street in broad daylight.

Tattooed on his right forearm, a gold fist
wreathed in green laurels.

He hands me his favorite VHS tapes:
Five Deadly Venoms, Drunken

Boxing, Fist of Legend.
I watch all eight in two days.

He gives me shirts that he says
will fit me perfectly.

His favorite joke: five knuckles
buried in my rib cage.

Sometimes, he hits me so hard
I forget where the sky is.

I wake in his chest.
I wake mid-fall.

Mercy sweet throat.
Mercy chocolate milk foam.

When he takes us to other states
he buys us cheeseburgers and milkshakes,

tickets to horror movies that
never stopped haunting me.

He knows the circumference of his boys' skulls
by heart. Their hats, the first thing he snatches

off their heads. Their sleep eyes, their Coca-Cola
teeth. He shows us how to get a number

from a waitress at Hooters instead
of a bill. It's no surprise when I find

three exclamation marks and no
commas—his sentences lit

like a nightclub on its slowest night.
He strings them together carelessly.

As if made for me, he hangs each one
around my neck.

Tony Gloeggler

Holiday Music

When the guy next door,
yells out, *You think I'm happy*
the baby cries louder.
I am surprised not to hear
either of the dogs barking,
the wife cursing back.
I turn my music louder,
Laura Nyro's *Christmas*
Beads of Sweat for New
Year's Day. I flew home
from visiting Jesse yesterday.
Nearly twenty years since
I spent New Year's Eve
with him, his mom. Happy.
I remember he was sleeping
and we were in bed. Straddling
my hips and laughing, small
town city hall fireworks flashed
through the window, across
her eyes. The guy throws
a couple of fucks against
the wall and the woman
hits him with a son of a bitch.
These days we hardly talk.
Emails to arrange, confirm
monthly visits. We rarely
raised our voices, but the strain,
the silence, strangled the breath

out of the room. Something
bangs against the wall, shatters
across the floor. The husband
screams again. The Northeast
is frigid and that makes everything,
me, feel lonelier. Sometimes, I miss
Jesse's mom, even though I know
day to day we never fit that well.
A door slams and I hear footsteps,
paws, scuttling down the hall.
I love Jesse and miss him
as soon as I leave, but realize
how much easier my life has been
not taking care of a special-needs kid
moment to moment. I walk
to the window, watch snow fall.
The woman-next-door's face
is hidden behind the hood
of her fur-lined parka. She's trying
to pull the leash tighter, smoke
her cigarette, unfold a tiny plastic
bag and bend to pick up two
piles of crap before it stains
the new fallen snow. I go
into my bedroom and before
I close my eyes, I hear a lock
unlatch, the guy next door's
even tone, *Feel better now?*

Ross White

There's a Void and It Needed a Villain

I hate the word "lovers," its farce
      as a too-intense moniker.
What passes for love is often just a volcano,
      a sweatshop, an overheated engine.

I say things all the time to overstate my case,
      as if argument were a form of glue
but opposition a kind of lubricant
      at a time when I'm desperate not to fall apart.

"Lovers" sounds a lot like "lemurs"
      but lemurs become quite comfortable in captivity.
A good lover cannot quite be trapped,
      or if confined, will rattle the cage,

too unruly to be properly cared for.
      The temptation is nonetheless great.
When I stare at glowing ember atop ash,
      I always imagine wrapping my palm

around the fleeting pulse of its orange.
      Every good idea needs a companion.
In captivity, lemurs adapt to use tools,
      a behavior never seen in the wild.

They need constant stimulation.
      The tools prevent tension and aggression.
The moment after you called me "lover,"
      I could sense myself becoming its opposite:

a damp towel, a submarine, a truncheon.

Laurie Blauner

We Can Talk About That

I listened to ice melting in Iceland, a dessert fork flung against a plate, the hoarse noise my old stray cat makes when he wants to go outside, a personal earthquake rattling down our street like a truck. Still the world can shrink to a country, a state, a street, or a kitchen. A neighbor, who forgot her mind, once said, "It's nice that you're here, in the park with me." We were standing in her old, yellow, crooked kitchen that seemed to be dissolving in the afternoon light.

Loss and redemption has fur. Having lost one cat and gained another, I stumble onward, learning how to wander, avoiding the homeless people living under a Seattle bridge near me. A man, who speaks to himself, not into a device, erects a complete bed with an iron frame, frayed sheets, covers, and a lumpy pillow. The man has long, stringy hair. He smiles. Holding out a dirty hand, he says, "Here's a room where my heart was." A woman, with a face like a leaf, wearing a crocheted shawl, sits on her pile of clothes and bedding with her pant legs spread apart, under noise and small light from the bridge above that opens occasionally. Sometimes a muscular bonfire burns, its arms reaching high into the air.

Many things I imagine don't come true, a swarm of bees emptying out a favorite restaurant so I can dine undisturbed, or lightning pointing in an expedient direction. I embrace imagination, some odd animal dangling from a tree branch, which, without my intervention, could fall and create a life of its own.

There is the economic value attributed to a life through a wrongful death lawsuit (someone's earning potential) or the value of a statistical life, as in: How much more to spend to save how many people? See the tobacco, auto, workplace, healthcare, clean air, or transportation industries. In the U.S. in 2008, $50,000 is the equivalent amount of money for one quality year of life (*Time*, "The Value of a Human Life, $129,000," Kathleen Kingsbury, May 2008).

How much is an animal's life worth? What a human wants to spend on it.

Possessions:
- a serious green striped jacket on someone's shoulders
- a train moving slowly to gather a last look at yellow corn, chattering geese, and trees knitting themselves together above a river
- quick, white wings that throw gulls into the air
- emptiness that I try on when you are gone
- singing into a vast silence of knotted clouds
- doing arithmetic in the middle of winter
- the defeated rise not thinking about themselves
- what I am I leave

Disturbed Dictionary

My mother's fur coats are made up of various parts of sharp-toothed animals. She has three different types: mink, fox, and something exotic I can't name. All of them need to be packed into cool, dark storage in the summer. Furs require breathable cloth, not plastic bags. They need space and no direct humidity or sunlight. As clothing, they are more mausoleum than zoo.

It's fall and the animals at the Seattle zoo, in their contradictory pastorals, are being fed their inscrutable futures. The Northern Trail area is jealous of the warm, steamy African Savanna or Tropical Rain Forest or Tropical Asia. The various sections of the zoo are the Trail of Vines for the orangutans, apes, monkeys, and a chilly, rugged landscape for bears, otters, goats, and owls, and an Australian type of habitat for kangaroos and emus. Birds are contained inside the enclosed Willawong Station, fluttering everywhere, landing on a shoulder or arm. A dome in the Tropical Rain Forest helps keep the vegetation inside damp and sweating. The Temperate Forest, which is similar to Seattle's landscape, contains Asian cranes, pandas, wolves. Life is a theme park.

I'm lonely at the zoo, watching a litany of flamingos leisurely fighting, furtively fucking, momentarily gliding over water with their passionate orange-pink and white feathers. They flap folded wings, stand on one impossibly long, slender leg, survey their scumbled enclosure while the sky unfurls over them. They are consumed with petty divisions, fights, and alliances. I think of my mother's words this morning, *never* nested close to *enough*, and all that's passed between us without beaks or claws or webbed feet. I remember the flamingos' large, pale eggs from last summer and wonder what the birds have grown into. I wonder at their wanting.

Our eyes lock between glass, the orangutan's and mine. She's in her exhibit, vines, earth, trees, torn burlap bags, and I'm in mine, cement, signs and explanations, artificial lights. Mine is temporary. Her eyes contain old ideas, upward and downward scenes, shadows and moonlight, overturned meat and scavenged vegetables, frayed, secretive objects, sunlight and unweaving the woven, scratched and smoothed fur, long grass tipping every which way, something frightening at night. Her dreams must be faster and more visceral than mine. We study each other's bodies and faces and slight movements. I speak, simply saying *Hello, beautiful.* No one else is there. She languidly looks at me, perhaps waiting for more words or waiting for nothing more than time to pass. I press my palm against the glass in front of her, and it is a long time before she raises her own, quickly taps the glass with her fingertips then turns to leave.

Tired women, usually in groups, are pushing strollers, disturbing leaves, which are collapsed everywhere. Small ambulatory children are excited, racing toward glass windows filled with animal antics or emptied landscapes. I'm sad for the lonely black-and-white tapir, a creature to himself, and I'm glad for the companionship between two hippos, whose backs surface regularly like giant, amiable rocks. At the Petting Farm, goats, with their blank, startled-yet-accepting faces, are positioned on tabletops to nibble on twigs held out to them by volunteers. Pigs are writhing in hay, fancy chickens are pecking at soil. Strange miniature horses stare at their fences, and a rabbit, made of muscle and fur, waits curled patiently.

Vestiges of animals remain in me, like the desire to swat an insect at my knee. My cloud-white bones test their hard testimony. Fur is no longer visible, usable limbs, the belief that I'm talking only to myself, circling round and round my favorite places before I lie in them. I feel danger on the surface of circumstances, share incipient eyes, heads, hearts, and a reliance on scenery. We are more alive when fighting, yet none of us likes lions racing toward us out of nowhere. When I come home, I notice crows, hummingbirds, and gulls, cats and dogs, gray squirrels, possum, raccoons, frogs and insects, wondering exactly how they belong to us.

Forgotten Constructions

I'm lifting my spoon repeatedly from hot soup to my mouth on a cold day. Pale, round stones fill my mouth. I'm shoving moons between my lips like a wolf. I'm lucky, eating when I want. A house surrounds me, shifts, stirs, and I'm safe from what roams the Earth. I'm a flawed human, Hominin clade, using tools and complicated clothing, a strangled or robust fire to cook my food, with art and technology to express myself. At Halloween I usually dress as a black cat, flimsy velvet ears on a headband, a dark raggedy tail pinned above my buttocks. One quick motion and my costume flies off. Mostly, we've forgotten where we come from in our push to inhabit and relegate.

Totems:
- I have become lost in a spider's web, the gelatinous, stringy material washing my hands, but I'm afraid of the tiny, devious spider.
- The hummingbird hovers, wings beating frantically to disintegration, a monosyllabic noise, because we are curious about one another.
- I want to make something of myself in the water, fish nudging me, but I keep losing myself.
- I'm watching a crow fly far in the chilly weather. Whose sky is it?
- I pick up a hard-shelled insect from a used plate in my kitchen and place it back outside.
- I see the bear roaming a Montana hillside. I'm glad for the distance between us.
- The frog's body fills with noise, releases it like a girl who has put her packages down.
- I unscientifically come to a precipice to see what the eagle sees.

- The suspicious elk, embedded in a contagious darkness, worries about the unreliable things moving around him.
- I want to make something out of something else.

"Species dysphoria" affects people who believe they were born in the wrong species and can feel phantom limbs, claws, tails, or wings. They are creatures trapped in a human body. They think about flying, burrowing, swimming, jumping, climbing, and running, so that they can leave their shapes and shadows behind. They can be too large or awkward playing with balls or balloons, ascending stairs or ladders, fetching a necklace or chewing on it. Or so small they want to believe they can fit through a mouse hole or the space beneath a door. Ceilings and floors know nothing. These people reuse their hands, mouths, feet. An open window changes its meaning. Relevance is learned from swallowing clouds and depositing them at the feet of the woman who calls you home using your pet name. This is a place you like, with goat hearts beating under the moon, inviting grass to sway, hiding behind a ropey tree, twisting toward light. Evening seems more important than morning when you are mindless and tired and the landscape is full of relevant gestures. You rehearse who you are, someplace you are welcomed.

I gather beauty, which sometimes thinks only about itself and, if collected and seen in the right way, inspires joy, as if there could possibly be more beauty. But to get there, I need to be as reckless as a beast, enjoy the possible and move forward. I need to watch for dogs that swarm menacingly from a periphery, refocus on my intrusive illusions and my unlovable ideas. My mind trespasses through the broken window of a house to discover what is precious on someone else's desk, a heart packed in ice, a story set against the animal kingdom. Mine is the same window, house, and desk. We are all related although we see things differently through the kaleidoscope of our various experiences. Some of the things I imagine do happen, like seeing pelicans excited about fish, a smoldering fire on a beach on a winter night, stars smiling as darkness arrives, the radio reciting. I'm always alone although there are sometimes people around me, my husband and a friend or two, and animals, especially animals. I'll always ask why. I'll always be shocked and amazed by the world. I need to wonder what happens without exactly knowing why or who. Who will change? We can talk about that, too.

Ellen Stone

Hand me down

Worry, a kernel—
seed my mother's
mother sewed
in her breast pocket.
Kept there, lightly.
Just over her heart.
Gray tweed jacket,
woven of cardinal
feather, shredded
sky, cinders.

Passed down.
Fitting sure as
clouds fill gaps
in blue. Sleeves
of doubt. Collar
shrugged. Bleak
weather, a sure
prediction. *You
look just like
your mother.*

Scarlett Peterson

Frivolity

God help the man or woman who marries
this decorated wreckage.
I am not a lamb.
No, I am a goat in a flower crown,
pissing in my own face and eating your debris.
You only love me for the tidiness I leave behind.

Scarlett Peterson

Dismemberment

I'd like you better split in two—
half the body I grew used to holding
only mine—
the other half hers,
and never within reach.

Half of you, like that baby in the Bible,
and I the selfish woman
with no child of her own,
willing to let you be torn apart
for me—

so that, in the end
you won't go home to her either.
I would go before the king and say—

*I earned this love,
and I'll bury what's left.*

Tammy Delatorre

The Baby Garden

1.

    The tomato plant has wrapped its tendrils around the wire cage that descends into a hoop-style skirt. The plant resembles a woman; heavy fruit droop from her torso, evocative of lactating breasts. Jacob wanted to keep the back yard mostly grass—for the kids, always so single-minded toward the next phase of our life. When he was courting me three years ago, persistence was part of his charm.

    I reasoned with Jacob that fresh produce would be a healthy addition to our kitchen and managed to lay claim to a small corner of the yard for a garden with a lemon tree, herbs, cucumbers, and tomatoes. I snuck in the roses, our one allowance for a plant with no utility.

    From the garden, I see Jacob has come home. He is a shadow pacing the kitchen. He's gone to look at the chart tacked onto the refrigerator with a large red-letter A magnet. On it, I record my daily body temperature, cervical softness, and vaginal discharge. Today, there's a stringy consistency and eggshell color; all signs indicate an optimal moment for conception. He reminds me of my father, who checked the lunar and tidal charts to read the right timing and tide to pull fish from the sea.

    Jacob has stopped pacing and now stands at the kitchen sink. Any moment, I will be called inside to do the thing that couples do to create new life, so I hurry to the rosebushes in full bloom and thorny. I hold the shears but cannot make the cut. This is where I lost them, the babies, all three of them. The doctors told me to stay engaged in calm, nurturing activities. With the sun and fresh air on my glowing cheeks, I bled into the soil. My blood mixed with the water and nitrates that feed the roses and tomatoes. I sniff at a nearby rose and hear a baby's heartbeat in the petals.

Jacob has come up behind me, hands at my waist, lips pressed at the nape of my neck. "Hi, beautiful," he whispers into my ear.

My shoulders tense up. The garden feels too small for both of us. Plus, he doesn't understand about the gardening and the bleeding, the failures endured by my body, flushed from my womb, babies in various stages of completion, pink fingers, puffy bellies, and big, round eyes. I'd rather he wait inside.

"You need any help out here? Look at that one." He points. I see the large heirloom, bulging with ripeness.

"Should I pick it?" He bends down without waiting for an answer.

"No," I put my hand over it, unable to shake the thought of the tomatoes as breasts.

"I can get it." He kneels. The tomato at eye-level now.

"You always do that."

"What?"

"Treat me as if I'm in some delicate condition or something."

"That's not what I was doing."

I pluck the tomato and it fills both my hands.

"It's a brute," he says.

I can tell he wants to touch it. "I don't want it to bruise," I say and carry it into the house. He follows behind.

Inside, his eyebrows rise and fall. "Hey, the chart looks good."

I nod, wishing I had a moment longer, just me and my tomato.

"Baby-making time."

I cast a disgusted look his way.

"I mean, you know, whenever you're ready," he says and opens the refrigerator.

I remember his appointment. "Did you go in today?"

"Yes, but we should still try the old-fashioned way."

"What did they say?"

He doesn't answer right away but then smiles broadly. "My guys are strong swimmers." He looks back into the refrigerator, unable to find something appealing. "The count was a little low but nothing boxers and loose jeans won't fix."

"How low?" I close in and feel the cold air escaping.

"Doctor says it's fine."

I stare at him.

"It's on the low end but not abnormally low." He searches my face to read how he's offended me.

I nod. "Right. Then it's not your fault."

"I didn't mean it that way. I'm just glad that out of all the things it could be …."

"It's not you." I stare at the tomato. "Which means it's me."

2.

Infertility treatment is supposed to be the cure for those ailing in the baby-bearing department, and I am ailing on the scale of five miscarriages now, maybe more, but that's the confirmed number.

Perhaps the problem is the aging of my eggs or rusty fallopian tubes. The doctors momentarily cast a suspecting eye at Jacob. But with all the hormonal treatments and procedures I've had to endure, he simply squirts into a cup and is cleared.

The hormones came first in pill form, taken every day like fertilizer for the soil. Next, it was the needleless syringe, commonly referred to as the turkey baster. I am awake for the procedure, and when I see the actual device, it doesn't look like a baster at all. Instead, the small plastic-metal plunger resembles the pistol plug aerator my father and I used to thrust into the lawn, pull out little tampons of soil to give the roots space to breathe and expand in springtime. And that's what I try to think of: The soil in my belly has become compacted, as if around a taproot. The doctors must go in and make room.

"Abigail, lie back," they say. I think of compressed clay; the root won't move no matter how hard they pull. Breathe, they say and heave again. Gentle at first, but now it's time for the spade, anvil, and hoe— to get at it. Clear space.

"Abigail," the nurse gently shakes my shoulder. "You must have dozed off."

I wake, vaguely remembering a dream of gardening tools.

3.

After the artificial insemination doesn't work, the doctors produce an actual needle. Guided by ultrasound, they make their way into my ovaries to harvest eggs.

Of all the things my father taught me about growing a garden, there was never a need to go back in and extract seed. We always used the little packets. There was the one time I watched him graft orange trees, cutting young stems into matching, adjoining Vs and taping them together. They were forced to grow, one to the other.

When I get home, I scour the internet for gardening tips but find this article about a girl who supposedly got pregnant from a blowjob. The guy, some unsuspecting one-night stand whose seed was so strong it survived the gastrointestinal tract, digestive fluids, and expulsion from the other end. The girl's enticing pheromones called the sperm to cross the short desert of her skin to the vaginal canal, where it found and fertilized an egg successfully embedded in the uterus lining. *They can't make this stuff up, can they?*

I put the computer to sleep and go to the kitchen. I take out the two red vine tomatoes sitting in our garden basket and put a large heirloom in their place. I wrap a dishtowel around its baby-soft skin and rub its red belly. People don't understand that gardening takes patience, a lot of silence and compassion.

4.

I sneak a peek down the aisle with baby clothes. It's the section of Target I have no claim to. I want to run my cart down this row just to touch the soft, white, cotton onesies, to pick up the boxes with tiny booties and matching mittens, to read and chuckle at all the cute phrases scrawled on blue and pink bibs. But I can't go down that aisle. The real mothers have surrounded the circulars and end-displays. They hold up baby clothes with judgmental eyes. Is it the right size or color for baby?

I'd be happy to buy any of it, to browse even, but I cannot be around those women right now, who take motherhood for granted, myself such a failure at this basic female function, and if even one of them were to ask after my child, as if I had one, I'd crumble to the floor, sobbing. I've lost so many now.

All the items on my shopping list have been checked off except Jacob's last-minute request for socks—the request was made this morning when he saw me making the list. I made the list after I peed on a stick and was given a positive pink reply. I'm pregnant, but I'll probably just bleed this one out, too. Into the garden. They seem to be aborting themselves earlier now. So, I didn't tell Jacob the news.

Among the racks of men's T-shirts, briefs, and boxers, my cheeks go hot with fury. I've been down this aisle before. I grab a package of short ankle socks in an assortment of colors, when I know full well Jacob likes calf-high whites. I sneer at the thought of the sock slipping down to his heel, his trying to dig it back up and keep it in place.

I meander through the rows of home furnishings, shower curtains, and stainless-steel cookware, too early to go home, so I make my way to the cleaning supplies again, justifying that an extra box of disposable dust sheets for the Swiffer sweeper is probably a good idea. How can society, including me, be simultaneously determined to save the planet but have no problem consuming large quantities of convenient disposables? This is the type of misaligned thinking Jacob always misses and cares not to acknowledge even after I point it out, because then he'd be forced to see his complicity in it. Me, I'm good with unwarranted blame. I take the long way, past the baby aisle again, this time spying a plastic tub for bathing, tiny sponges, honey-colored shampoo and pink lotions.

There are fewer women now, so I begin to load up with one-piece bodysuits, pull-on pants with footsie art, microfleece sleepers, Sherpa hoodies, striped terry outfits, and cuffed socks. I grab things quickly and indiscriminately because I don't want to get caught trespassing by the real mothers. I walk out of Target with two large bags of baby items.

5.

When I arrive home, Jacob has left a message that he will be home late from work. Out in the garden, I pick the large beefsteak and heirloom tomatoes then the smaller varietals. Instead of washing them in the kitchen sink, I place them in the brand-new baby basin. I take the basin into the bathroom, lower it into the tub, and fill it with warm water.

I use a soft terry washcloth to lather soap onto the fruit. This is how it would feel with the heat and steam dampening my hair, knees and back beginning to ache as I bend over and wash my child. The hooded towels come in handy to wrap the tomatoes I picked and now carry cradled against my breast back to the bedroom. I lay them out on a swaddling blanket. From the Target bag, I select a yellow, one-piece sleeper. Using the Romas, I fill the limbs, use the larger beefsteak and heirlooms to make up the torso, and snap everything snugly into place. I remove the rubber bands from my hair and tie off

161

the suit at the wrists so the tomatoes won't fall out of the sleeves; the legs have enclosed booties.

I stand back to view the little one. Something's missing. Back out in the garden, I pick a large, blooming pink rose, sniff at it before I clip the stem, and, oddly, it smells like the head of an infant, sweet-milk sweat and talcum power. I insert the rose stem into the neck of the jumper, extending so long it reaches into the leg.

I close my eyes and pick up baby. It has the right weight and feel against my body. I pace and bounce the infant in my arms. This is how it would be to rock and comfort a child until she's ready for sleep. I place my baby back on the bed below the pillows and spoon my body around hers. The rose head rests below my chin. It took all afternoon to make baby when I should have been cooking supper. I should have been taking my body temperature and marking the rest of the signs of fertility on the chart, but instead I made baby.

"You're just what I always wanted," I whisper into her flower head. "I love you so much."

I fall asleep and dream of baby, now real. Its skin is so soft, hair like the sensitive tendrils of a bashful fern. I am playing with the child on the bed. This tiny, precious girl dressed in yellow and lying on a blue blanket, and my baby is so new she rarely opens her eyes, and the skin of her eyelids is a translucent pink. But in the dream, Jacob comes home and scowls at the child—its nose is too wide; ears, too large; and hair, so sparse it has no eyebrows. I curl my body around baby to shield it from his view because it would never be good enough, but the tomatoes shift. I wake to find Jacob standing on the other side of the bed.

I look down. The tomato body has become malformed during my fitful sleep, and its rose head, squished beneath my chin.

"What are you doing?" Jacob comes forward and picks up the rose head, which has detached from the body. Pink petals fall to the floor.

I try to catch the petals as they fall.

Jacob reaches out to touch my arm but hesitates. I try to gauge the intent in his eyes, but the room is dark.

He sits on the edge of the bed, the baby between us, and puts the flower head back in place. He snaps the undone button over the baby's belly. The yellow nightie is spotted pink with tomato juice; torn petals lay around it like little eyelids. I try to remember my dream. Was this my baby? "She'll take ballet," I murmur.

Jacob puts his hand on the tomato belly. He bends down as if he'll pick her up, but I swipe her up in my own arms. I feel the wet blotch on the baby's back, a runny, red trail bleeds down the sleeve of my white blouse. Jacob spots the Target bag on the floor. He grabs something from it and hurries down the hall. I hear the sliding door to the backyard. I run out after him. He's taken the wicker basket and is picking more tomatoes. Still holding baby, I rush over to stop him, but he's picked the green and yellow fruit until the branches are bare. He goes after the cucumbers too young to harvest and drops to his knees, his back toward me. When he's done, he sits on his haunches. I draw closer and realize he's made his own baby, this one in a pink, floral jumper. The preemie cucumbers have made good arms and legs. He's used a red rose for her head.

I approach him slowly. He smells of the garden, mint and sage. I put my hand on his shoulder. "She'll run track," he says.

My eyes tear up. I didn't know he wanted a girl, too.

He looks up at me, unsure. "There are other ways we could do this."

I place the baby I am holding down so they lie side by side. I squint; they could be our children. I think I see their chests rise and fall. For the first time in a long time, I allow Jacob to caress my thigh, realizing his touch is for his own sorrow and comfort, not mine.

Mary Schmitt

Job Speaks to Betty, the Organizer of His Book Tour

I sank a wide bowl of wine inside me, Betty,
at the reception after this reading. I don't blame *you.*
Tonight, you gave me a well-mannered crowd.

They turned off their cell phones without being asked,
sat up straight on their trim American behinds.
The women cried softly at the harrowing parts,
when I read the verse about the deaths of my children.
And now you have your own book, named after you,
said someone when I'd finished reading,

then came the turn that always startles me, applause,
followed by the signings, the hearty sales.
I smiled my thin smile of nervous relief as I signed
and sold.

I need a cauldron of gold, of debit card treasure,
to maintain what God gave after my long wail of loss:
the new holdings and herds, the new scatter of children.
I have to strike my wordy flint while the iron is red;
I don't think I have another book inside me.

As I said, a deep bowl of wine tonight, a pit,
at the afterglow. My dead children's faces, pale,
unripe berries, kept showing themselves to me,
then the face of my faraway wife, her own pallor,

☾

her stunned enormous uncomprehending eyes.
She called out *Be still* to our children
as they moved between the tables piled with wine
and platters of pricey vegan wafers,

their legs flashed like moving sheep shears,
playing their children's game of hide-and-seek.
A game without shouting, or echoes of laughter.
Just the spin of their small churning legs.

You're a clever woman, Betty, a kind one.
Perhaps I can find you a good husband
among my tribe of new acquaintances.
Because you were born to have children,
Betty, with those big ship-bell hips.
I want to give you presents, gifts with meaning,
goats or a man or a tied bundle of something,

because you book my readings

because I like to watch the sway of your hips

because you listen to my drunken babble
without sighing or opening your lips,
just with your cupped hand molded to my shoulder

when I tell you about my quiet brutal nights
after my first set of children died,
when I knew I could only love again in a numb fumble,
behind a cloud or a groan or an acre of wine.

I stared up at the cold stars for hours, Betty.
Brutal and quiet; goddamn you, God, yes.
Stared at stars broken off from pattern. Constellation.

Mary Schmitt

Watching Hills, and the Trees

On walks, my husband used to point out the best spots to post snipers,
his eyes claiming the pretty, growing swell of hills. The tips of trees.
Listen—even our boys were small then. It was usually in the late fall,
after we'd picnicked, the leavings of our simple meal, the little boxes of
   juice,

tossed in an outdoor bin. At the woods' edge, stillness, then boys' feet,
barely skimming the curl of dead leaves on trails. We would follow,
my eyes moving with the arc of my husband's index finger, stretched
   toward sky.
His sniper stories were both like and yet not like his other stories of
   Da Nang,

the ones about endless trees running down the sides of mountains
   until they bent,
bowing to the South China Sea, the French nun he'd known who ran
   an orphanage,
kept a Tommy gun slung around her neck. He used the same earnest
   That was me
tone of voice for the sniper, the nun stories, the emerald trees falling
   with female grace

into the sea stories, though the sniper stories carried their own hard
   thumbprints,
their own step over the edge into falling, falling. Still, fingers on the
   same hand.
Green lift of a tree branch in wind, lookouts posted to shoot, the nun
   with her rosary,
her matter-of-fact ways, her bullets. The wife and kids coming along,
   not much later.

Allison Wyss

Boobman

So let's get the big question out of the way right off. I'm that guy you see riding through town on a bike, all in spandex, with a poufy, blond wig and boobs like helium balloons. That's me, Mike Chesterton. Why? Because I feel like it. It's just what I do.

I'm also an electrician—the perfect job for me. I mean, it's long, impossible days and often tedious, tracing wire to wire to wire. But there's glory in it, too. Just think, I take a dark house and light it up. Some day I'll get an emergency call, in the middle of the night—then I'll be a real hero. And, in the meantime, it's good money.

What does my wife think about my hobby? The boobs? The bike? She thinks I'm a little odd, but it's not a big deal to us. Patty does some strange things, too. Like undressing in alphabetical order. Like running her flip-flops through the dishwasher.

Just about every day, after work, I drive to Peter Park and hide the car behind the shack that serves as public restrooms on the forgotten side of the park. Then I strap on my gear, pop the boobs into orbit with a shoulder twitch and a pelvic wiggle. The wig suctions into place and I clamp it down with a sprinkling of bobby pins. Spandex hugs my thighs, whispers at my chest, statics up my backside. Swing the bike from the trunk and I'm off. The best part of my day.

Today, I'm spinning, as usual, over the winding asphalt of Peter Park, bike zipping underneath me. The wind whips and whirls at me, tugs at my extremities, tickles my torso, while the whiz of the bike twists at the pavement. Trees and flowers and mothers with strollers all warp into bright and unusual shapes. The landscape on a bike. It's open air, so you can really see. Look sideways and the colors run together and smear close up. Skateboarders swoop then stretch out backwards with my movement. The kids that chase me, running or skating or pedaling bikes—even their words spiral, so I can't hear them. Faces smirk, but it's clown smiles when I pass them, harmless.

Then the zips, when I get to the edge and can peek into windows of houses that butt up against the park, a fraction of a second to glimpse a slice of a person and then imagine their whole life. A woman on the couch. A man lunges toward a dog. A little boy kicks a little girl. Just a flash, a slap, maybe I didn't even see it. Far away, the perspective changes. It's still and smooth. The trees line against the horizon. The playground slide is still against the sunset, sharp and straight in its stand-up form.

After a couple of circuits, it starts to get twilight-y, so I pump my way back to my phone booth, balloons in front of me bumping up and down, one and the other. A shift in my hips and the whole pattern changes. They bump together and apart. Thighs burn, vibrations juicing through me. I swing the last swooping corner to the clearing where the restrooms sit.

Today, it's like there are diamonds on the ground. The grass is like a lake when the last rays of the sun hit it, glimmering, sparkling, flashing. I'm confused. I jerk to a stop, unclip my feet from the pedals, and dismount.

It's my car's windshield, shattered on the ground. Must have been those kids. Smeared over the back side of the building is "BOOBMAN" in neon-pink spray paint. So, yeah, it's those kids.

The satisfaction that must come from smashing a windshield, the spark of pure joy in the thrust, the crack, the explosion of glass pebbles. The car is insured and there's nothing inside worth stealing.

I change into my day clothes then call a tow truck and get the driver to take me home along with my bike and the gym bag of hair and boobs and spandex.

I'm like a dog hanging my head out of the tow truck window, feeling the wind, watching the shapes and remembering the boobs bouncing above my bike tires. Huh. Boobman. I like it. It's better than "he-she" or "manimal." It's better than the queer or the freak or the sicko. I'm Boobman. Like a superhero or something.

My hop gets springy as I kick down from the tow truck, boobs bouncing in the gym bag on my shoulder.

"What happened to the car?" Patty, my wife, is running water over some frozen cube steak and must have seen through the window when the truck let me out.

"Smashed windshield."

"Did you hit something?"

"Nah, it was parked behind those old bathrooms where I change clothes."

She pulls her hands up, bright pink, from under the water and wipes them on a towel. "Mike! Who would do that?"

"It's those kids, I think."

"What kids?"

I haven't told Patty about the way they chase me in the park, the names they scream, in spray paint, on the side of my changing booth. Until now they haven't been much of a problem, and even now, I don't want to make it a big thing.

"Some kids hang out there, I think. I see their beer bottles and cigarette butts around."

"This is just where you change clothes, right?" Patty is flipping the towel around in her hands. There's a tassel on the end that she picks at. "Maybe you should change at home."

"Would that bother you?" I've always tried to keep my boobs out of the neighborhood so as not to embarrass my family.

"The kids are gone." Patty picks up the thawing meat from the sink and squeezes it in both hands. "It will be safer for you to change at home."

Maybe Patty's right. With the kids grown up and out of the house, it's time to bring this home.

What does it feel like? My bike in the wind? The orbs bouncing? The hair streaming? It's kind of like Superman, I guess, when I'm really flying.

You know how you wear that little white skirt to play tennis? Or how you wrap that belt around yourself for karate class? It's the same thing with me and the boobs.

Patty doesn't like to tell people what she does for a living, even though she's an accountant, a CPA. What's to be ashamed of in that? It's the quirks that make me love her so much.

And Patty will slap me sometimes—that's odd, right?—when she's in a particular mood. Flat, open hand on the ass or on the meaty part of my leg. She does it for the sound, she says. It does make a nice smacking-sucking-reverbrating twang but only when she places it just right.

I wouldn't try to change anything about Patty. I couldn't make her better than she is. Also, it's not my place to, not my business, if you really think about it.

It's the next day and I'm at the front door of a new client, one Mr. Thomas Klacken, who found my ad in the church bulletin and wants his basement wired. The door opens before I can ring the bell, and a tall man in a suit almost steps right into me. His shoulders twitch, maybe, or maybe not, it's so quick, and then he says, smooth as anything, "Morning," and nods at me.

"Mike Chesterton. I'm the electrician," I say, but he's already passing by, liquidly, with the same motion letting me in the house. "Talk to my wife," he says.

There's a bony, youngish woman in the front room, stooped, picking up bits of something from the carpet. She stands when she sees me but doesn't say anything right away.

"Mrs. Klacken?" I keep my hand in my pocket in case she doesn't want to shake it. "Mike Chesterton? Electrician?"

"Yes, I'm Melanie Klacken." The woman wipes the back of her hand against her forehead, looks at something over my shoulder, and then looks at me. "Hi." She smiles but just barely.

She leads me down to the basement, which is sort of half-finished—concrete floors and bare drywall, slapped up in a hurry. There's a single light bulb hanging from the ceiling above a washer and dryer and a couple of boxes in a corner but nothing else. She takes me around the room to find the pencil marks her husband has made on the walls. "The seller tried to call this a finished basement. Well, we're finishing it now. Let's see, Thomas marked it … yes, light switch here and then outlet here … here … here …." Her feet are bare on the concrete floor and make a horrible dry sound as she shuffles from wall to wall.

Melanie Klacken seems antsy as I set to work in the basement. She climbs up and down the stairs repeatedly, runs laundry up from the machine, digs through one of the boxes, offers me glasses of water. She doesn't trust me there by myself. Eventually, she brings that same basket of laundry back downstairs and starts to fold it. I get a look at the top of her head, mostly. Her white scalp is stark where the hair parts in a jagged line. She's got on smudgy makeup and sweatpants with a drawstring cinched so tight it hurts to look at her waist and the pinch of skin poking just over. When she leans, to reach for a sock or whatever, her shirt slides up her back. There's something dark there, maybe a bruise or else a large birthmark snaking across her torso. I'm curious, if a little disgusted, so I watch her carefully out the corner of my eye. She tucks the T-shirt into the sweatpants, forces it in even tighter against the drawstring.

"So I think I've seen you somewhere before." She has a high, nasally voice.

"It's church, St. Chuck's. I've seen you there with your husband."

"Oh, yeah." She holds a towel clamped at her chin and her arms make big wings of it and flap them together. "Sorry I didn't recognize you. We just moved here in March."

She goes upstairs then. Maybe she trusts me after mentioning church.

It's good that she's gone because I have to adjust some of her husband's Xs. I keep as close as I can, though, and he seems to have known mostly what he was about in marking them. Without any more distractions I put my head down and get at it. There's no reason I can't finish this job today. Pliers in the hole, needling, stitching, wrapping, whirling. Tight and shred it out in frazzled, ribboning ends. Wire to wire to wire. Clamp and twist.

I'm making really good time until some peculiar ravel of wire winds through my fingers and into my brain. There's something vicious there. Also, it reminds me of Bruce Road, that twist of asphalt that will sweep me to the park this afternoon. I feel hot breath on my calves and kids hooting at me. So, mid-fish, I choke. I can't get the thread through. Wire dead-ends in the wall with a rasping thud. My arms are scraping at the rough hole in the drywall; I'm reaching further and further, up to my shoulder. The clean edge I cut, around the hole, is crumbling. But fuck good form at this point. Fifth attempt now. Sweating, breathing hard. My heart's going into a panicky little flutter-beat. I'll try once more, I decide, then finish this job up quick. So I pull the fucker up, stretch my arms, and wiggle my fingers. I walk a lap around the basement before starting again. It finally fishes clean.

I feel better once I get home and dressed. It's exhilarating to emerge from my own house, for the first time, all dolled up, where people can see me, instead of from that nasty little building in the park. When I toe-walk down my driveway, I prance a little, click-click in my clip-in shoes. I'm a whipped-up torrent of blond feathering up top, round and wild and shoulder-width, then a bubble—two bubbles—of perfect, round, bouncing fullness. A quick taper to solid torso, narrow hips. My legs diminish to a point at my sharp-arched, extended feet. I tiptoe down the driveway, electrically, a little too perfect. I can't handle it long and it's a relief when I hop on the bike, which balances me out, neutralizes the too-perfect shape by grounding wheels to my bottom half.

So, changing at home, I have to ride my bike to the park, take this twist of a thruway, Bruce Road. I've had my eye on it for a while, as it's deliciously smooth and winding. It's a three-mile stretch of asphalt, two lanes in each direction, that coils up and out of my neighborhood, tight to the city, then swings in a big, looping curve, cutting through cornfields, out to the airport, before wrapping itself right up to Peter Park, where the cars can't follow me. There's no sidewalk but a grassy ditch on either side and an aluminum guardrail down the middle. Speed limit is 35 but not many keep to it. It's a glorious stretch for a bike. The fields, flat, but leaves rolling in the wind, knee-high corn like an ocean. Blurred at the edges, where the sky hits the ground, but fuzzy because of distance. The telephone poles, on the other hand, nearby, and the flowers in the ditches, those are blurred from movement, power lines coursing-swelling-stringing, from my pedaling through space.

Then into Peter Park, and it's a perfect day for my bike. Except there's one odd shape that keeps recurring as I circle the park then again and again. It's that flash of darkness, coiling up a bright-white torso.

When the sky starts to color, it's time to head back over that marvelous twist of Bruce Road. There isn't traffic right now. I let go of the handles and let my arms spread wide. Thin wisps of air run through my fingers like electrical wires, fizzing smoothly in sharp, tiny currents. I have a little bit of sixth sense in peddling my bike and running wires—I'm not exactly psychic, but there's just this feel to it, life stringing through me and connecting me to the world.

A car pops out of the horizon behind me and quickly catches up. It's these kids. They're slowed to my pace now, creeping behind me, tailing me closely. I realize they don't get older, somehow, as the years go by, always same kids. The same as run or skate or bike behind me in the park. Now it's six of them packed into a station wagon borrowed from one of their moms. Their bumper breathes on my calves. They honk and scream or maybe just laugh. I can't understand words at this speed, but I get the gist. The secret is to stay steady, keep going, don't look sideways. Soon they'll veer off or else speed up and zip by. Shit, I can't panic—a wobble could kill me. They zip past.

I don't think the kids mean any harm. It's just a joke to them. But I wish they'd leave me alone.

I don't take this, the boobs, anywhere but on my bike. I don't wear ball gowns or tutus. Never pantyhose or high heels. Only cycling gear. Only the hair, the breasts, the spandex. A swipe of red lipstick. But only when I'm riding.

I sometimes think about growing my fingernails out. I imagine the wind would pull at them, creep underneath, tug me in one more way, feel just a little bit more on my bike. But I keep them short for Patty. Sex with Patty is gentle, painfully soft, and overflowing with sweetness. Claws would ruin that.

They're not really balloons, of course. Balloons would pop too easily. Hit by a piece of gravel thrown by a truck or something. I don't want an explosion out there or even a slow leak.

After my ride, I shower and come downstairs just as Patty throws her car keys on the kitchen table. I'm shirtless, so she tweaks a nipple as she kisses me on the forehead and asks about my day.

"Patty, you know how I get feelings, how I run from wire to wire and know things that I don't have any business knowing?"

Patty is flipping through the mail. She throws up her arms, a bill clutched in each hand. "You're not psychic!"

"What about that time at the lake? With the Kraussmans' dog?"

"You've got good instincts." Patty tosses down a stack of envelopes and opens up a circular so it unfolds and blocks her body.

"Whatever you call it, you know I got it." I sit down at the kitchen table and fold my bare arms in front of me.

"Maybe."

"Maybe?"

"OK. You know things sometimes. You figure things out."

"Well, this asshole I just did a job for, I figured out he hits his wife."

"Oh, God."

"Yeah."

"Is she OK?"

"She hides it. Won't talk about it or admit anything."

"So you don't know for sure."

"I'm sure."

"Well, if she doesn't say …." Patty has re-folded the advertisement, stacked it with the other junk letters, and is chewing on her fingernails. She pauses to take her hand from her mouth and poke at a hangnail, thoughtfully. "If she won't say … I don't see what anybody can do."

"I know. It's just a shame."

"I feel horrible for that woman," Patty says.

Patty doesn't mind my biking gear. Just like I don't mind her quirks. Patty, she talks to dinner sometimes. I walk in and she's lecturing a pork chop or cheering on the mashed potatoes. "Little mini-pizza," she says. "Now, why won't you slide off this cookie sheet and listen to me?"

Mostly, Patty and I don't talk about my habits, because what is there to say? She'll sometimes offer advice, out of the blue, about how to tie back my hair, and when there's a sale on gear, or if the roads are slick with rain. But mostly she leaves me to myself about it.

What do my friends say about my getup? They say—well, there's a couple other guys, electricians like me, that I get beers with once in a while. They don't say anything. Jim, an old friend from high school, we have him and his wife for dinner sometimes, and I'm not sure, really, if he even knows. We're not so close anymore. I was in the Kiwanis club, which was great—I got to help people, be a sort of hero. But I quit last spring because I never really fit in. Those guys were all businessmen or salesmen. They wore suits every day. I don't have a lot of friends, I guess, but I don't need them. I've got Patty and my kids. I've got my bike and my job.

It's cooler this afternoon on my bike even though the sun is out. Colors are sharp, shapes are smearing gloriously. The air currents wrap around and underneath my boobs, circle the balloons, spin off, cross at my breastbone. The wind sucks at my wig, pulls it back and up, tugs at the clips that hold it in place, and nestles between the nylon and my real, buzz-cut scalp. Cold air in my teeth feels like a toothpaste commercial.

I'm shaped like a speeding bullet—pointed toes, tapered legs, then large and full up top. Or maybe I'm an arrow and my curls are the feather on the shaft.

I pedal hard and fast and take the curve at a slant, the wind rustling up my bangs. On Bruce Road, I ride top speed. There's just a flash at the edge of my vision—a truckload of kids. I feel them more than see.

These have been the same kids for thirty years, haunting me on the roads and in the park. My nemesis, you might say. But, really, they don't mean any harm.

I hear the yell, "There's the queer!" stretched out in the air, tickling just past my earlobe and twisting up into the tendril that blows there. I slide to the shoulder but keep my speed. The truck screeches and swerves at my rear tire. Just to scare me. Doesn't hit, but it's close. I catch a lungful of air behind my boobs, a sharp stab in my chest. Still up and peddling furiously. The truck should pass me now, so I keep exactly on the line, the edge of the asphalt, before the road drops into gravel then ditch. The kids stay behind me, laughing down my neck. Shit. I bail. I tip myself off to the right, tuck my head, and tumble head over tires, down the ditch. Through my legs, I catch a sharp flash of smile, maliciously stretched over open teeth, one of those damn kids, laughing at me.

I'm fortunate to be armored in padded boobs and a helmet of hairspray. I've only scraped an elbow, and my bike is fine. So I wait a minute then straighten out my chest harness and straddle the bike just as another car pulls up on the shoulder. What are the odds? It's Patty in the Taurus.

"Mike! Oh, my god, what happened to you?"

I clap a hand over the elbow scrape. "Just stopped for a breather."

"Here?" Patty is out of the car and scrambling up to me. I prop myself at an odd angle, one foot half-clipped into a pedal, arm twisted around myself.

Patty pulls something from my hair. "What is this?" It's grass. "And you're crooked." She tugs at my wig, one hand over each ear. "You fell."

"Yeah, I took a little tumble."

"Are you OK?"

"You bet. Just a minor spill."

"Oh, my God, it was those kids." Patty's voice gets louder and a bit shrill. She jerks harder at my wig. I lose balance and spike my pedal foot at the ground, but Patty doesn't let go. "Those damn kids. They passed me earlier, going way too fast."

She takes her hands away from my ears and uses them to hide her face, which is getting awfully pink. "Are they the same ones?" She gulps air. "In the park, with the windshield?" She bunches up her eyes. "They're chasing you on the road now, aren't they? Aren't they?"

"Eh."

"Jesus Christ, Mike!" Now she's tugging at her own hair. "You're going to get yourself killed!"

"Patty, you're over-reacting." Bruce Road is not the place for this discussion. And anyway, I'm fine. "Can we talk about this later?" I click my pedal-foot back in place. "After my ride?"

"It's my fault you're on the road—oh, my God—but that stupid bathroom—it's not safe, either." There are big tears bubbling in Patty's eyes but not overflowing. "Will you please come home now?"

"Just a short ride. Once through the park."

"Mike, I want you to get in the car."

"Once through the park. Please? I need it."

"I want you to get in the car."

"Fuck, Patty. Fine. Open the goddamn trunk." I slam my bike in, slam the trunk, and then slam the passenger door after I climb in. We don't talk the whole ride home. I just pull off my wig and play with the curls.

My boobs. I'll tell you they are soft and light and bouncy. And firm and solid and pretty much unbreakable. But, no, I won't tell you what they're made of.

Patty hasn't forbidden my riding—not that she could stop me, if it came down to it—but I should give it a day before I go back out. Just to be safe, just to respect her opinion. So the next day, instead of taking my bike out, I go for a walk. The houses in my neighborhood look different at the slower pace. More square, the corners are sharper. I'm watching shapes, winding through my neighborhood into the next.

I reach the Klacken house. It's dark out and getting chilly, but the inside of their kitchen is lit. Just him and her, sitting at the table, eating some sort of chicken out of a casserole dish. I can't hear them, but I see their mouths open and their heads tilt back.

I walk around the block so I don't have to pass the house again on my way home. My shadow is ahead then below and then behind me as I walk between the streetlights.

I'm still craving my bike when I get home, but it's too late at night. I don't put on my gear. Instead, I give the bike a wash in the driveway, in the dark. Warm bucket of soapy water. Suds the seat and handlebars, wipe the frame, scrub the tires. Then a blast with the garden hose. Looking at the bike, hooking my thumbs in the spokes, and thinking about tomorrow, the shapes warping, and the wind, and my full, bouncing breasts—it cheers me right up. Tomorrow, I'll take my bike on patrol.

No, I don't shave my legs. I don't have to shave my chest or back, either, in case you're wondering.

Do I wear panties? Well, that's getting awfully personal, don't you think?

It's the next day, after work, and I'm feeling bold in my boobs. It's a good day to circle the surrounding neighborhoods, let myself be seen, maybe swing by the Klacken house again. I wait until it's almost dark to ride down the Klackens' street, wait until Mr. Klacken will be home from work. I slow to a crawl when I reach their block. It's harder to balance at a slow pace, and the boobs are swinging far to the left then far to the right. There are two silhouettes in the window, him and her, a sudden hard gesture, but I'm past too quickly to be sure what it is. I make a four-block circle and am approaching their house a second time when a car peels from their driveway. It's him inside, the triangle of his shoulders a dark shadow through the windshield.

I drop the bike on the lawn and click-clack to the door, which opens as I get there.

Melanie Klacken's head is down, her hair dragging in front of her eyes. "I'm glad you came back."

"Miss?" I shift from one foot to the other.

She looks up then and gasps. She takes a step back. "I thought you were —."

"It's Mike Chesterton, the electrician?" I pull at my wig, but the clips are secure and I only manage to tug it sideways. "Don't mind the … I saw … through the window … I thought you might need some help."

She gasps again and steps forward. "What did you see?" She looks past me at the street. "Oh, God, come inside, please." She shuts the door behind me.

"It looked like —."

"It's not what it looked like." She sits down on the edge of the couch then stands right up again.

"OK." I look at her for a minute then swipe my wrist across my mouth to get rid of some lipstick. I wiggle the wig harder and when it finally peels loose, I pocket the clips and hold the curls in two hands.

"Oh, god. Dinner." She moves through the living room to the kitchen and I follow. My shorts are riding up a bit, so I give them a good yank when her back is turned. The boobs are still hovering nicely, floating front and center, juicy and round. With both hands I pull down on them, hoping to smoosh them lower in my halter top, but there's no flattening these babies.

She's got one pot of water on the front burner of the stove, in a noisy boil, and another in the back, with a lid covering what smells all tomato-y. Her back is to me as she dumps a box of dry lasagna noodles into the water. "Sorry," she says. "Thomas will want dinner when he gets home."

"Smells good."

She seems to be relaxing as the boil builds back up in the pasta water. "What exactly did you see?"

"Not much, really." My bike shoes click on the floor when I step forward. "I just have a suspicion."

She mumbles "suspicion" in a low, under-her-breath whisper. Her elbows press into her sides. She's got a big spoon in her hand, which she squeezes then lays carefully on the counter. She pivots on one heel to face me again. "I'm sorry. Why are you here?"

I look at her for a minute, building up my nerve. I'm searching for a mark on her, something to steel me. Nothing on the arms or neck. Her legs are covered up by jeans.

Then she looks right at my wrist, the smear of red lipstick crossing it. She is silent and stares at it for a little while. "Did we forget to pay you?" she says finally.

"No, it's not that." I take a breath, watch the water curl over and over in that pot on the stove. "It's your husband. You can leave him. I know he hits you." Every syllable thuds in a careful enunciation.

Mrs. Klacken stands with her mouth open for a moment, then she turns to the stove and pokes into the pot with that big spoon.

"There's this shelter, the women's shelter, it's pretty nice actually—I know where it is, because I used to be in Kiwanis and we went there once to bring them stuff. They'll help you out, at least with the first bit. Or maybe just give you some time to think ...."

Mrs. Klacken pokes harder into the pot of water then leans her face over it until her head is lost in steam. Her hair dampens and hangs over the pot like dark, wet noodles.

"I can take you there. We can go right now if you want. Before your husband gets home." I biked here but figure she'll want to take her own car anyway, and Patty can pick me up later.

She turns around to look at me, her face and hair all steamy. "What the hell are you talking about? Get out of my house."

"I know he hits you."

She slinks down a bit, cowers, so that her back is curled and her shoulders are high against her ears. "I'll call the police." Her voice is high and strained and her body pulls tighter, tenser with the words. Steam has turned to watery rolls, creeps down her cheeks to swing, dripping off her chin.

"Come to the shelter with me." I take a step toward her and reach around a boob to slink my hand out to her.

She flinches, bounces back and away from me, toward the stove and knocks her elbow on the boiling pot, hard enough to make a splash and a sizzle. "Shit." She claps her other hand over a quick-blooming burn, shakes the arm tensely, and chews on her bottom lip.

"Are you OK?" I jump another step toward her, but she darts sideways out of my range.

"I'm fine. You should leave." Her voice is even higher now. "Before my husband gets home."

She twists her arm to see the burn, which is red and shiny, gives a little hop, then she blots around it with the tail of her shirt. I am between her and the sink, so I step out of her way and let her grab a towel, run the arm under cold water. When she steps past me, her shirt is still pulled up in back and I can see a bruise now, a green one, nebulous, hovering above her waist. But her shirt drops and it's gone again, quickly.

"He hits you."

"He does not." She leans far over the sink to get the elbow under the faucet, so I go ahead and jerk the bottom edge of my shorts down with one hand, trying to cover another inch of thigh. My other hand pulls up tight on the strings around my neck so nothing pops out the front of my shirt when I lean over.

"I just saw the bruise on your back."

"There's no ... so what?" She turns to face me—I straighten—then she's focused again on the water running over her arm, dripping the length of it, onto the countertop and splashing the floor. "Why don't you mind your own business?"

"I just want to help."

She pulls her arm from the sink and shakes it. "Do you really think I'm going to leave this house with someone like you?"

"I could change clothes." My shoe clicks on the floor, rattles, then stops, and I hold still.

We're facing off then, staring straight into each other's eyes. She's got a fierce look to her, skinny and shiny-faced and hair all frazzled.

Then a loud and sudden fizz as the water on the stove boils over. "Shit." With the towel, she lifts the pot off the burner and right away dumps it through a colander in the sink. The pasta rolls out in a sticky, overcooked wad. "Shit." She lifts the colander from the sink and dumps the lasagna clump into the garbage then looks up at me. "You should go." When she looks up again it's at my chest instead of my face. She's lasering a hole in the right orb until I turn away and click-clack from the house.

I've scooped my bike from the yard and walked it to the edge of the block when Mr. Klacken drives past, pulls behind me into his own driveway. I put my head down and cross the street. Then I button my wig into place, clip in the shoes, and wobble out of the neighborhood. It's much later, and much darker, than I ever stay on the road, but I need some wind tonight, something to lift my spirits, remind me what Boobman is all about. There are no headlights on my bike, but it has reflectors. And Patty has sewn reflective strips into my spandex.

So instead of winding through the Klacken neighborhood into my own, I loop to the edge and dump myself to Bruce Road. I'll ride over this stretch then fly through the closed and darkened park.

I'm back alive on my bike, in the wind, boobs rolling and curls billowing. The shapes are dark but dragging out sideways, morphing into new, elongated, or quick-skinny forms. The lights are sharp pinpoints at some distance, globes of yellow fire from others. The zip of the road, the wash of headlights that come upon me then leave me dripping with reflected light.

Halfway down Bruce Road, flying over the smooth asphalt—there are the kids, heading the opposite direction, approaching fast. I give them some room, take the shoulder, and hold steady. They'll see who I am since the lights are good here, frequent, and bouncing off my curls, yo-yoing over my boobs. They take a swerving swipe at me but nothing more. I hold steady but feel lopsided, pulling so slightly off-center.

There are no cars on the road after they pass. I take the left lane and hug the center guardrail, spinning around the last curve, feeling my way into the wind, riding the street lights.

Then there are the kids behind me, out of nowhere. I don't know how they got turned around so fast, what with the guardrail. From the left lane, I can't bail into the grassy ditch, have to hope they mean no harm. They're on me quick. I try to hold but lose my nerve, my fault, wobble right, so slightly, and catch the front bumper with the outside point of my ankle, the rubber angle of my shoe. I knock off-balance and tip over the guardrail. Bike flips up, tires still spinning. A bra strap catches on the metal and snaps loose. Head hovers against the ground. I tuck in then. Cartwheeling hands and something scratchy at my face. Two rotations, maybe—it's hard to tell. My wrist tangles in the spokes for a second before the bike tears free and flips the rest of the way across the road. My bike catches the wind like a dark sail and lifts up up up then drops into the black ditch.

If I'd just held steady, those kids wouldn't have nudged me over like that.

I pick myself up. There are only a few tatters of skin left on the outside of my calf and thigh, but it doesn't feel like any bones are broken and I can walk, if I go slow. The orbs seem intact but squeehawed and jiggling out of rhythm. They're lopsided from the wallop they gave to the ground, and the harness straps are twisting out at odd angles. My head is cool and tingly in the fresh air, since the wig ripped off with the bike. It's crushed, so I wad it in my cleavage. A truck blows through and sprays a shower of dirt, dust, and gravel. I look down at my leg exactly once and then decide to keep my eyes up.

The wheels won't turn on the tangle of metal that used to be my bike, so I scrape it about two and a half miles along the shoulder of Bruce Road and then six blocks to my house, chalking out a dark smear on the sidewalk. The wind whips over the street and fluffs up a few hangnail tatters of skin on my calves.

Patty is still up. After a gasp, "Mike!" she sits me down on a kitchen chair then pulls my foot up on another. I pick at the wig in my hands, pull grass and pebbles from the curls, while she sponges my leg with a warm, wet cloth. Dirty, bloody water pools beneath us on the linoleum. I pull my focus back to the wig, twist it around my fingers. Patty has tweezers out, pulling stones and tar and grass and glass, ever so slowly, from my thigh.

"I can fix the wig, too," she says. The curls are hardly blond anymore, they're matted with so much dirt, and hardly curls anymore either with my pulling at them. "Just let me take care of this leg first."

I keep squeezing the wig with one hand as pebble after pebble comes clear in the silver tips of her tweezers.

"OK, honey." I say. "I love you."

"Also, Mike, I'm a little bit worried about your wrist. Is it OK?"

I notice that my left hand is hanging at an off angle.

Patty puts her hand underneath my wrist but doesn't quite touch it. "I'm almost done here. Then we'll head in and get that looked at."

I nod, and, with the movement, it's not my wrist that feels off but my shoulder. The weight is not right; it's uneven. I twitch and twist, subtly, try to ease back into place.

Patty looks at me, then her mouth opens and her eyes widen.

I feel a whiz, a current, a wetness. There's no noise, just a silent suctioning. I look down at my chest and my bony knee emerges, slowly, just behind the sculpted nip then pops all the way into sight as my right boob shrinks, sags, and then flaps, empty against my belly. The boob is blown, popped, defeated, dripping down my side, destroyed.

Laura Ponce

Paulina

The rows of cars move forward and stop again before the checkpoints. It's still dark and the drizzle beaded the windshield a while ago. It's freezing inside the bus. Paulina checks the time on her cell phone: Six in the morning. Taking too long, she mutters under her breath. She wants to pee. The blows on the window startle her. The door snaps open and two armed guards climb aboard. Like the rest of the passengers, Paulina rolls up her sleeve so they can scan the tattooed identification code on her right forearm.

When the barrier rises, the bus starts rolling forward, passes under the sign that reads: "Welcome to the Autonomous City of Buenos Aires," and climbs up the highway. Paulina doesn't look over her shoulder, because she knows that the checkpoints and the river are behind her. She feels a kind of intimate satisfaction as she does every time she enters the city, but she doesn't allow herself to be happy. Still too early for that, she thinks.

On her trip she watches the well-kept parks, the clean well-lit streets, and the towers built during the Nueva Etapa, and thinks about those who live in them. She remembers what her mother has repeated to her to the point of exhaustion: "There are two kinds of people: those who live inside and those who live outside. Those who live outside are allowed to enter only to work in waste management or security." Actually, it's the same thing, Paulina tells herself with a bitter smile, because those of us who work in security are also hired to handle waste. She remembers the man they had to take out, the one who every day passed by her post in the hall of the building without looking at her, as if she weren't there, until the morning when his ID didn't pass through the reader. Paulina rose to her feet, hung her baton on her belt, and approached him.

"Is there a problem, sir?"

"Yes, I don't know what's going on. It doesn't verify my ID." The man was sweating.

"Allow me," she said.

"Julio Montero/Section Chief." The man in the photo was him, everything looked in order, and the magnetic stripe didn't seem damaged, but the access reader again rejected it. Paulina knew what was happening. So did the man, although he didn't want to accept it.

"Wait, please," she told him.

She pressed the button on the radio asking for backup. Méndez had just thought of going to the restroom. She pulled out her reader and scanned his ID card. When out of the corner of her eye she saw Barbieri and Soto coming out of the elevator, she confirmed, "You are no longer employed by this company, sir. I'm going to have to ask you to leave the building."

The man said that it couldn't be, that there must be an error. He shouted, threatened, and begged, but they threw him out on the street. In the end, before leaving, he had a lost look and an expression that made her shudder. Everyone looks that way in the end, but she never got used to it.

It's been a while since she was last in the access post and other guards are the ones handling those cases, but Paulina often recalls that expression so she doesn't forget how easy it is to fall from where you are, how easy it is to lose everything.

She gets off the bus at the corner of the beach and checks her cell phone one more time as she walks toward the building: Six-thirty. She is on time. As she goes up the front stairs, she sees her reflection grow larger on the walls decorated with the NEC logo.

Peretti, the companion she will relieve, is in the office next to the access post. They exchange greetings, the usual phrases. "Is it cold?" "Yes, atrociously cold." And the news at the security firm. "A light bulb on the fifth floor burned out. Everything else all right?" "Yes, everything is all right." The twelve screens in front of the desk don't deny it.

Paulina goes to the restroom to change and comes back wearing her uniform. It's tighter each time, but the loose pullover and the jacket help her hide it. She signs the duty log and starts her shift. Peretti already has his bag ready, nods, and leaves. Now Paulina is in charge of the branch office, which means that the other twenty guards on the shift are under her responsibility. She takes the radio and starts checking the security cameras to see if they are in their posts and ready for the change of the guards.

At seven sharp she calls the company to confirm the attendance and pass the list.

Nothing happens for nearly two hours. The whole building seems suspended in silence. Then the company's employees begin to arrive in droves. Paulina entertains herself watching them fill elevators and swarm in the corridors until they fall into a routine. She starts to think today will be just like any other day. Then she feels it again. It's not exactly pain, it's something else, a kind of signal. And she can't ignore it anymore.

She goes into the restroom and splashes water on her face. She repeats to herself that she needs to calm down, that everything will turn out all right. She looks in the mirror and does not like what she sees: dark circles, those marks of bitterness ... anyone would say that she is forty-five, although she still has not reached thirty. The hairdo doesn't help either, she tells herself with a grimace, and lets go of her hair. She feels like crying.

She returns to her post just in time to see, through the mirrored window, someone greet the two guards at the access post. Judging by his uniform, he's the company's supervisor. Her heart flips over when she realizes who it is. A moment later he comes into the office.

"Good morning, Santoro."

"Good morning, Martínez."

And they kiss each other on the cheek.

Daniel Martínez has been her supervisor for years. Paulina still feels attracted to him. She's always enjoyed his company. Any other day she would invite him to stay, she would offer him mate or coffee, but today is not any other day.

"Any news?" he asks as he flips through the log.

"No, nothing," she replies, and in an effort to stop looking at the wedding band on his ring finger, she notices his impeccably pressed uniform. She observes his thin face and notes his receding hairline and his gray mustache. He's getting old, she thinks tenderly, and she has to suppress the impulse to stroke his hair. Suddenly she feels the weight of his absence, realizes she misses his embrace (anyone's, actually). She remembers the nights they spent together, the first and the last, and she's invaded by a sudden wave of heat, a confused mixture of fever, shame, desire, and bitterness. That's why she doesn't like to remember, because in the end, as she does every time she thinks of him, she feels stupid. She knows she doesn't' even have a fighting chance. She grits her teeth and, trying to finish off the procedure, asks, "Did you bring the coverage? Barbieri was asking if they exchanged francs …."

Alone, Paulina closes the office door, sits down carefully, and pulls up her pullover. She cautiously touches her belly. It's not very big, but it's already thirty-eight weeks. She has been hiding it for so long that sometimes she herself needs to touch it to make sure it's not her imagination. And there it is again, that pain that is not pain. Paulina already has a son—Marito, the "souvenir" her only boyfriend left her before disappearing—so she knows very well what she is feeling.

Restless, trying not to think about everything at stake, she takes her purse and starts preparing things.

That's when her bag of waters breaks.

Paulina breathes in, breathes out, and waits. There comes another one. It's like a big hand twists her guts from inside … and then releases them. She's seated on a couple of towels, leaning against the cold wall of the restroom, and she's controlling as best she can with the mirror she brought. She resists the desire to moan until she thinks she sees the crown, just then moans with all her might. She tries to remember her first labor. She prays to God that it's just as fast, prays to God that it does not come out feet first, that it does not tear her, that it breathes well, that it's complete, that it does not have any health problems. All the fears she did not allow herself to feel during her pregnancy suddenly invade her. And what if she couldn't do this alone? What if she needs help? But it's too late to think about that. She tries to empty her mind of thoughts and fears, tries to focus on her breathing. She moans once more and the head comes out. The hardest part is over, she says to encourage herself.

And the truth is, it ends up not costing her so much.

It's a girl. A baby girl with strong lungs. Paulina cuts the cord with a cutter and cleans and wraps the little one. She dries the baby's face, removes the bloody clots from her hair, and stares at her for a moment that seems eternal. She rubs her finger inside the baby's mouth, sees that she has a reflex, and brings her closer to her chest. When she feels her suck, her tears fall. She thinks about how things were before getting a job in the company, the endless rows and the endless rejections, sneaking into the cold shack where she slept, hunger as a constant pain. She thinks about her parents, those miserable, selfish old people who live off her. She thinks about her son, that fickle, ill-bred animal who does nothing but demand things from her. She thinks about the rent and the bills that need to be paid …. What would happen if they fired her? What would happen if she lost everything that has taken her years to acquire for this? It'd be worth it, she murmurs. And then she hears someone open the office door.

She has barely discharged the placenta and is lying in a large pool of blood.

Paulina wakes up in the clinic, in a pleasant modern room. She feels that her body hurts for everything that did not hurt during her labor. It's as if her organs and even her bones tried to return to their positions before her pregnancy. When she tries to sit up, she realizes she's handcuffed to the bed.

"Your work permit has been revoked," she hears a voice say. "As soon as you are discharged, you are deported."

She turns around and sees him sitting by the window. Daniel seems very tired.

"You know pregnancy is just cause for dismissal. The company could even take legal action against you for hiding information."

Paulina runs out of breath. He rubs his eyebrows.

"I know how much you need work and I'm doing everything possible to keep you from getting fired. There could be a position at a roadblock on the highway …. But I don't know."

Paulina thinks about what he offers her: the booths on the edge, rotating twelve-hour shifts, out in the open, armed—no one gives you a weapon for nothing—checking people, waiting for looters.

"And I will never be able to go back?" she barely manages to say. She refers to returning to her goal, the post she occupied, but actually she also refers to returning to work in the city, being with him again, and returning to everything that has made her life miserable and bearable until then.

"No, I don't think so," he replies, and goes to the door. But he comes back, as if he couldn't stand the fight.

"I don't understand how you could do this," he says. "I'm not only talking about keeping it secret …. Having her like that!"

"You know what would have happened if I had asked for a doctor when I broke down. They would have put me in an ambulance and thrown me on the other side of General Paz."

"They would have taken you to the hospital!"

"On the other side of General Paz!"

"That's why you didn't call? Why did you want her to be born in the city?"

Paulina doesn't answer.

"What did you think? That they were going to give you citizenship, too? You can't be so silly! They can give it to her, but not to you. You don't understand?" He throws a folder and a pen. "They offer you two options: Leave her in the care of the city, giving up all parental rights to the child, or renounce her citizenship and take her with you."

Paulina didn't expect it. She had come to believe she had a chance, that it wasn't such a crazy idea after all. She opens the folder, but can't read, the letters are blurred.

"There is no other option?"

"No, there isn't."

She thinks about it for a moment and the thought of separating from her makes her feel a choking, a sudden discomfort. She feels pain in her nipple, from which she fed her baby. She feels her breasts full and desperate, longing. She understands leaving her would be like undergoing an amputation, but she knows there is really nothing to decide.

"Tell them I give up parental rights."

He looks at her as if he's seen a monster and leaves the room. Paulina knows it's useless to try to explain to him and lies in bed. She remembers when she found out she was pregnant, when she decided to keep the baby. She remembers how she promised herself that everything would be different this time. She then told herself that it would her chance to start over, to do everything right from the beginning, to feel motherhood not as a shame, a burden or the consequence of a scam, but in that sweet and serene way you see in the movies, to feel and give all the love that mothers are supposed to have for their children. And she came to believe that she could really leave everything behind, that her life after childbirth would be as new as that of the child.

Things didn't go as she would have liked, and yet … yet, she feels this madness has not been in vain.

In spite of everything, her daughter will become a citizen. And no one can take that away from her.

A wave of sudden pride surges in her chest.

—Translated from the Spanish by Toshiya Kamei

Sophia Starmack

The Mess

It lived in the mess of two-by-fours and poison ivy
by the dog pen long collapsed, chicken wire,
clash of bent nails on the edge of the yard.
Its leash dangled between the trees.

It wore a baseball jacket, had so many arms it carried off
all the sticky bottles from the gas station at once.
It lit a cigarette, cracked a lid, sucked down the light
from my first floor bedroom as I pulled off my dress,

shrugging at my mother's injunction to pull the shade:
dark night plus lit-up window equals a movie screen.
I knew it before it had a name—him.
I wanted to see myself in the reflection of its teeth.

I dare you to be real, I said to the world, to him.
And then it was real, and he wouldn't go away.

Kate Hanson Foster

Knead

You know this sound
by heart: the short
jingling confidence
of your car keys hurried
back onto the hook.
And the humiliated
shadow that enters you
again. This house
that shelters you—
sometimes it carries
you away in a net.
Sometimes you put
your hand on the faucet
just to watch cold water
rush down the sink. Go
ahead and latch the broken
screen door outraged
by wind. Pull dead
vegetables from the fridge.
Measure the day in dinner
bells, how many times
the dog shits in the yard.
Hold yourself up
like yesterday's daffodil—
a bloom before the spoil
and wither. Press
your fingertip into
the chip of the fruit bowl.

Knead

You were a new
melody once. The crackle
of a fresh-lit wick.
Fold the oil of your hands
into the bread dough—
the world is thick
with worn-out words—
you must knead as if
longing had a taste.

Lana Spendl

As God Intended

We sat round a wood table at the library every week and read letters from conquistadors to crown. Cannons and horses and men men men—sweat and beards and scars and forceful hands—and then that one nun who dressed like a man and ran off to the Americas and fought pirates on the way. She pulled up the skirts of women and grabbed their breasts and laughed hard and wet with other males. She cut someone's face. The fear of being discovered did not temper her. Life surged inside her like a water jet, and when pressed on one side, she shot out the other.

Contributors' Notes

Samuel J Adams lives in northern California, where he works with adults with developmental disabilities. His stories appear or are forthcoming in *Ruminate, DIAGRAM, Atticus Review, Monkeybicycle*, and elsewhere. He received his MFA from Bowling Green State University and was a 2018 writing resident at the Kimmel Harding Nelson Center for the Arts in Nebraska City, Nebraska.

Hussain Ahmed is a Nigerian writer and environmentalist. His poems are featured or forthcoming in *Prairie Schooner, The Cincinnati Review, The Journal, Nashville Review*, and elsewhere.

Rachel Barton is a poet, writing coach, and editor. She is a member of the Calyx Editorial Collective, edits *Willawaw Journal*, and co-chairs Willamette Writers on the River. Her poems have appeared in *Oregon English Journal, Hubbub, Whale Road Review, Cloudbank*, and elsewhere. Her chapbook *Out of the Woods* was released in 2017. *Happiness Comes* (2018) was recently published by dancing girl press.

Laurie Blauner is the author of seven books of poetry and four novels. Her most recent novel, *The Solace of Monsters* (2016), won the Leapfrog Fiction Contest, was a 2017 Washington State Book Award Finalist in Fiction, and was listed in *Book Riot*'s Great Big Guide to Wonderful Books of 2016. Her essays have appeared in *PANK, december, Sycamore Review*, and *Superstition Review*, among others.

Anthony Borruso has an MFA in creative writing from Butler University and has been a reader for *Booth*. He suffers from Chiari malformation and sometimes examines this in his poetry. He teaches composition at Butler

University and Ivy Tech Community College in Indianapolis. His poems have been published or are forthcoming in *The American Journal of Poetry*, *Mantis*, *THRUSH Poetry Journal*, *Whiskey Island*, and elsewhere.

Giuliano Bruno is an artist from Springfield, Missouri. He combines painting with other art forms to challenge the formal understanding of what painting is. Inspired by nature, where forces of destruction and creation intertwine, Giuliano's artistic practice balances different methods in visual art. Bruno has shown at Planeta Gallery in New York City, the Lodge Gallery in Portland, Oregon, and Millet and Hammer in Springfield, Missouri. He can be found at giulianobruno.com.

Dakota Canon's first novel, *The Unmaking of Eden*, won the 2018 Hastings Litfest Crime Novel Competition and was long-listed in the 2018 Yeovil Literary Prize and the 2018 Caledonia Novel Award. She's received mention in the Manchester Fiction Prize, the Writer's Digest Annual Short Story Competition, and the Brilliant Flash Fiction competition and has recent pieces, either published or forthcoming, in *Hobart*, *Literary Orphans*, *Fiction Southeast*, *The Citron Review*, and other journals.

Whitney Collins' fiction appears in *Ninth Letter*, *Grist*, *The Pinch*, *LUMINA*, and elsewhere. Her stories have been thrice nominated for Pushcart Prizes, and she holds an MFA from Spalding University. She lives in Kentucky with her husband and sons.

Jim Daniels' recent poetry books include *The Middle Ages* (Red Mountain Press, 2018), *Rowing Inland* (Wayne State University Press, 2017), and *Street Calligraphy* (Steel Toe Books, 2017). His next collection of short fiction, *The Perp Walk*, will be published by Michigan State University Press in 2019.

Tammy Delatorre is a writer living in Los Angeles. Her essay "Out of the Swollen Sea" was selected by Cheryl Strayed as the winner of the 2015 Payton Prize, and her essay "Diving Lessons" was awarded the 2015 Slippery Elm Prize in Prose and recognized as a Notable Essay in *The Best American Essays 2016*. Her writing has also appeared in *Los Angeles*

Times, Good Housekeeping, The Rumpus, Vice, and elsewhere. More of her stories and essays can be found on her website, www.tammydelatorre.com.

Ian Denning's short stories have appeared or are forthcoming in *The Guardian, Tin House*'s Open Bar, *Passages North, Washington Square Review,* and elsewhere. He graduated from the MFA Program in Writing at the University of New Hampshire and now edits fiction for *Pacifica Literary Review.*

Dana Diehl is the author of *Our Dreams Might Align* (Jellyfish Highway Press, 2018) and a collaborative collection titled *The Classroom* (Gold Wake Press, 2019).She earned her BA in Creative Writing from Susquehanna University. She received her MFA in Creative Writing at Arizona State University. Her work has been published in *North American Review, Passages North, Booth,* and elsewhere.

Michelle Donahue is a PhD candidate in creative writing and literature at the University of Utah, where she is Fiction Editor for *Quarterly West.* She has an MFA in creative writing and environment and a BS in biology. Her fiction has appeared or is forthcoming in *North Dakota Quarterly, Sycamore Review, CutBank, Arts & Letters,* and other journals. She is the current coordinator for Writers in the Schools for Salt Lake City.

Kate Hanson Foster's first book of poems, *Mid Drift,* was published by Loom Press and was a finalist for the Massachusetts Center for the Book Award in 2011. Her work has appeared or is forthcoming in *Birmingham Poetry Review, The Comstock Review, Harpur Palate, Salamander,* and elsewhere. She was recently awarded the NEA Parent Fellowship through the Vermont Studio Center.

Sarah Freligh is the author of *Sad Math* (2015), winner of the 2014 Moon City Poetry Award and the 2015 Whirling Prize from the University of Indianapolis. Recent work has appeared in *The Cincinnati Review, SmokeLong Quarterly,* and in the anthology *New Micro: Exceptionally Short Fiction* (W.W. Norton, 2018). Among her awards are a 2009 Poetry Fellowship from the National Endowment for the Arts and a grant from the Constance Saltonstall Foundation for the Arts in 2006.

M. Brett Gaffney holds an MFA in poetry from Southern Illinois University. Her poems have appeared in *Exit 7*, *Rust + Moth*, *Tahoma Literary Review*, and *Zone 3*, among other journals. Her chapbook, *Feeding the Dead* (Porkbelly Press, 2017), was nominated for a 2018 Elgin Award from the Science Fiction and Fantasy Poetry Association. She works as co-editor of *Gingerbread House* and writes horror genre reviews in her spare time at *No Outlet Horror Reviews*.

Tony Gloeggler is a lifelong resident of New York City and has managed group homes for the mentally challenged in Brooklyn for over 35 years. His work has appeared in *Rattle*, *Paterson Literary Review*, *Chiron Review*, *New Ohio Review*, and elsewhere. His full-length books include *One Wish Left* (Pavement Saw Press, 2002) and *Until the Last Light Leaves* (NYQ Books, 2015). His next book will be published by NYQ Books in 2019.

Melissa Goodrich is the author of the story collection *Daughters of Monsters* (Jellyfish Highway Press, 2016), the poetry chapbook *IF YOU WHAT* (Fourth and Verse Books), and the collaborative collection *The Classroom* (Gold Wake Press, 2019). She earned her BA in Creative Writing from Susquehanna University and her MFA in fiction from the University of Arizona. Her stories have appeared in *American Short Fiction*, *Kenyon Review Online*, *Necessary Fiction*, and other journals. Find her at melissa-goodrich.com.

Maggie Graber is a queer poet originally from the Midwest. She is a recipient of grants and fellowships from the Barbara Deming Memorial Fund and the Luminarts Cultural Foundation, and her poems have appeared or are forthcoming in *The Louisville Review*, *Southern Indiana Review*, *Hobart*, *The Adroit Journal*, and elsewhere. Most recently she worked as a Wilderness Therapy Field Guide in the mountains of North Carolina. Find her online at maggiegraber.com.

Jonathan Greenhause was the winner of both *Aesthetica Magazine*'s 2018 Creative Writing Award in Poetry and the 2017 Ledbury Poetry Competition. He was first runner-up in the 2018 Julia Darling Memorial Poetry Prize, and he earned second prize in Cannon Poets' 2018 Sonnet or Not Poetry Prize, as well as third prize in both the Cornwall Contemporary Poetry Festival's 2018 Competition and The Plough Poetry Prize 2017. His poems have recently appeared or are forthcoming in *Columbia Poetry Review*, *New Ohio Review*, *Redactions*, and *Salamander*, among other journals.

Amanda Hadlock is a graduate assistant at Missouri State University, where she teaches composition and creative nonfiction classes.

Joseph Harris' stories have appeared in *Great Lakes Review*, *The MacGuffin*, *Third Wednesday*, *Storm Cellar*, and elsewhere, and have won the Gesell Award for Excellence in Fiction, the Tompkins Award for Fiction, and Detroit Working Writers award for fiction. He holds a BFA from Emerson College, an MA from Wayne State University, and an MFA from the University of Minnesota. He lives in Detroit.

Kathleen Hellen is the author of *The Only Country Was the Color of My Skin* (Saddle Road Press, 2018), the award-winning collection *Umberto's Night* (Washington Writers' Publishing House, 2012), and two chapbooks, *The Girl Who Loved Mothra* (Finishing Line Press, 2010) and *Pentimento* (Finishing Line Press, 2014). Nominated for the Pushcart Prize and *Best of the Net* and featured on *Poetry Daily*, her poems have been awarded the Washington Writers' House Poetry Prize, the Thomas Merton Prize in Poetry, and prizes from *H.O.W. Journal* and *Washington Square Review*. Find out more at www.kathleenhellen.com.

David Herghelegiu is a senior at Missouri State University and is working towards degrees in creative writing and secondary education.

Dustin M. Hoffman is the author of the story collection *One-Hundred-Knuckled Fist* (University of Nebraska Press, 2016), winner of the 2015 Prairie Schooner Book Prize. He is an associate professor of creative writing at Winthrop University in South Carolina. His stories have recently appeared in *Baltimore Review*, *The Adroit Journal*, *Washington Square Review*, *Witness*, and elsewhere. You can visit his site at dustinmhoffman.com.

Donald Illich has published poetry in journals such as *The Iowa Review*, *Fourteen Hills*, and *Cold Mountain Review*. He received an honorable mention in the Washington Prize book contest. He recently published a book, *Chance Bodies* (The Word Works, 2018).

Jonathan Winston Jones is a social scientist working in government. In 2018, he won first place in the VanderMey Nonfiction Prize contest at *Ruminate* magazine. He is pursuing an MFA in creative nonfiction at Northwestern University.

Toshiya Kamei holds an MFA in literary translation from the University of Arkansas. His translations of Latin American literature include books by Claudia Apablaza, Liliana Blum, Carlos Bortoni, Selfa Chew, Leticia Luna, and Sara Uribe.

Sarah Layden is the author of the novel *Trip Through Your Wires* (Engine Books, 2015) and the flash-fiction chapbook *The Story I Tell Myself About Myself* (Sonder Press, 2018), winner of the inaugural Sonder Press Chapbook Competition. Her work appears in *Boston Review*, *Booth*, *McSweeney's Internet Tendency*, *Salon*, and other outlets. She teaches creative writing at Indiana University-Purdue University Indianapolis.

Nancy Chen Long is the author of *Light Into Bodies* (University of Tampa Press, 2017), winner of the Tampa Review Prize for Poetry. She is the recipient of a National Endowment of the Arts Creative Writing fellowship, a writer's residency at Ox-Bow School of Art, and a scholarship at the Provincetown Fine Arts Work Center. Her recent work can be found in *Third Coast*, *The Southern Review*, *The Adroit Journal*, *Ninth Letter*, and elsewhere. She works in the Research Technologies division at Indiana University.

BJ Love teaches English and creative writing at the Emery/Weiner School in Houston. His poems have been published in *Gulf Coast*, *North American Review*, and elsewhere. He is production editor at *Pleiades*.

Amanda Marbais' fiction has appeared in *failbetter*, *The Doctor T.J. Eckleburg Review*, *Joyland*, and many other journals. She has written reviews and cultural essays for *Your Impossible Voice* and *Paste Magazine*. Her short-story collection, *Claiming a Body*, won the 2018 Moon City Short Fiction Award and is forthcoming in March 2019.

Brianna McNish writes from Connecticut. Her stories have appeared or are forthcoming in *Okay Donkey*, *Jellyfish Review*, *Pidgeonholes*, *Hobart*, and elsewhere. She has also received nominations for *The Best Small Fictions* and the Pushcart Prize.

Loria Mendoza is a writer, curator, musician, and performance artist who lives in Austin. She earned her MFA in creative writing at San Francisco State University. Her work has been published in *The Acentos Review*, *Mobius*, *Fourteen Hills*, *The Walrus Literary Journal*, and elsewhere. Her book, *Life's Too Short* (Fourteen Hills Press, 2017), won the Michael Rubin Book Award.

Jonathan Minila's short-story collections include *Alto contraste* (Universidad Autónoma de Nuevo León, 2018), *Todo sucede aquí* (Ediciones Cuadrivio, 2017) and *Lo peor de la buena suerte* (Universidad Autónoma de México, 2015). He is also the author of two children's books: *El fantasma sin recuerdos y otras historias para niños extraños* (Planetalector, 2017) and *El niño pájaro* (Pearson Infantil, 2015). He lives in Mexico City.

Scarlett Peterson is a Georgia native who received her BA in English and professional writing from Kennesaw State University. She is working on an MFA in poetry at Georgia College. She is editor-in-chief of *Exhume* and assistant editor of poetry for *Arts & Letters*. Her poetry has appeared or is forthcoming in *FIVE:2:ONE*, *Ink&Nebula*, *FRiGG*, *The Magnolia Review*, and elsewhere. Her nonfiction has appeared in *Pamoja*, *Madcap Review*, and *COUNTERCLOCK*.

Born in Buenos Aires in 1972, **Laura Ponce** is a writer and editor specializing in science fiction. She edits *Revista PRÓXIMA* and writes a monthly column on women and science for *Amazing Stories*. Her stories have appeared in magazines and anthologies in Argentina, Spain,

Cuba, and Peru. Her first short-story collection, *Cosmografía general* (Ediciones Ayarmanot), was published in 2016.

Alyssa Proujansky has studied fiction in Ithaca, London, and New York. She was recently a runner-up in contests held by *Atticus Review* and *Psychopomp Magazine* and a finalist in *Third Coast*'s 2018 Fiction Contest. Her work appears or is forthcoming in *Passages North, Gulf Coast Online, Hobart, Lunch Ticket,* and elsewhere. Her website is www.alyssaproujansky.com.

Mary Schmitt is a Michigan poet and short-short story writer. Her themes include the complexities of family relationships and the healing power of nature.

Simon Shieh is a poet and the director of InkBeat Arts, an organization that empowers young people through artistic expression. He is also the editor-in-chief of *Spittoon Literary Magazine,* which translates and publishes the best new Chinese writers into English. His work appears or is forthcoming in *Grist, The Journal, SOFTBLOW,* and *Kartika Review,* among other journals.

Taylor Jim Sly is an undergraduate at Missouri State University. He lives in Springfield.

Lana Spendl's chapbook of flash fiction, *We Cradled Each Other in the Air,* was published in 2017 by Blue Lyra Press. Her work has appeared or is forthcoming in *The Cortland Review, Hobart, Notre Dame Review, Baltimore Review, Zone 3,* and other journals.

Sophia Starmack's poetry and essays have appeared in *Barrow Street, The Threepenny Review, Best New Poets,* and other publications. Her poetry chapbook, *The Wild Rabbit* (Deadly Chaps), was published in 2015. Sophia was a 2014-15 poetry fellow at the Fine Arts Work Center in Provincetown, Massachusetts, where she currently serves as writing fellowship coordinator.

Will Stockton's latest books include *Jesus Freak* (Bloomsbury, 2018) and *Members of His Body: Shakespeare, Paul, and a Theology of Nonmonogamy* (Fordham University Press, 2017). His translation of Sergio Loo's *Operación al cuerpo enfermo* is forthcoming from the Operating System. Other translations have appeared in *Kenyon Review Online*, *Waxwing*, and *The Chattahoochee Review*. He teaches English at Clemson University. Find him at willstockton.info.

Ellen Stone co-hosts a monthly, city-wide poetry reading series in Ann Arbor, Michigan. Her poems have appeared in *Passages North*, *The Collagist*, *the museum of americana*, and *Fifth Wednesday*, among other places. She is the author of *The Solid Living World* (Michigan Writers' Cooperative Press, 2013). Her poems have recently been nominated again for the Pushcart Prize and *Best of the Net*.

Cammy Thomas has published two collections of poems with Four Way Books: *Inscriptions* (2014) and *Cathedral of Wish* (2005), which received the 2006 Norma Farber First Book Award from the Poetry Society of America. Her poems are forthcoming or have recently appeared in *Tampa Review*, *The Ocean State Review*, *Compose*, *The Missouri Review*, and elsewhere. A fellowship from the Ragdale Foundation helped her complete *Inscriptions*.

Preeti Vangani is a poet and essayist from Mumbai with work published or forthcoming in *The Threepenny Review*, *BOAAT*, *Juked*, *Noble / Gas Qtrly*, and other magazines. She is the winner of the 2017 RL Poetry Award, and her first book of poems, *Mother Tongue Apologize*, is forthcoming from RædLeaf Poetry-India. She holds an MFA in writing from the University of San Francisco and lives in the Bay Area.

Virginia Watts is the author of poetry and stories found or forthcoming in *Burningwood Literary Journal*, *The Brushfire Literature & Arts Journal*, *Green Briar Review*, and *The Florida Review*. Her essay "Marti's Father" was nominated for a 2018 Pushcart Prize by *Ponder Review*. She received honorable mention in Passager Books' 2018 Poetry Contest.

Charles Harper Webb's latest collection of poems, *Sidebend World*, was published by the University of Pittsburgh Press in 2018. *A Million MFAs Are Not Enough*, a gathering of Webb's essays on contemporary American poetry, was published in 2016 by Red Hen Press. A recipient of grants from the Whiting and Guggenheim Foundations, he teaches creative writing at California State University, Long Beach.

Ross White is the director of Bull City Press, an independent publisher of poetry, fiction, and nonfiction. The author of two chapbooks, *How We Came Upon the Colony* (Unicorn Press, 2014) and *The Polite Society* (Unicorn Press, 2017), he teaches creative writing at the University of North Carolina at Chapel Hill. His poems have appeared in *The American Poetry Review*, *New England Review*, *Tin House*, and *The Southern Review*, among other journals. He is the editor of *Four Way Review*.

Allison Wyss' stories have recently appeared or are forthcoming in *Alaska Quarterly Review*, *Yemassee*, *Booth*, *Lunch Ticket*, and elsewhere. Some of her ideas about the craft of fiction can be found in "Reading Like a Writer," a monthly column she writes for the Loft Literary Center, where she also teaches classes.

Allyson Young is an MFA candidate at Syracuse University and an editor-in-chief at *Salt Hill*. Her work has been published or is scheduled to appear in *Bennington Review*, *Columbia Poetry Review*, *fields*, *Cosmonauts Avenue*, and elsewhere. Her chapbook, *The West and Other Mistakes*, was released in 2016 via dancing girl press.